Advance Pr~~aise for~~
Fairways to Le~~adership~~

"At the PGA TOUR Superstore and the First Tee, growing the game is an integral part of our DEI and community engagement initiatives. *FairWays to Leadership®* provides access to the game by utilizing a unique and creative curriculum that introduces young adults to the opportunities the game affords. The PGA TOUR Superstore will continue to support organizations such as FairWays to Leadership® in our effort to introduce golf and its inherent values to a more diverse and inclusive community."

> —**Rich Alvarez**, *manager, community engagement and philanthropic giving, PGA TOUR Superstore, and volunteer coach-mentor, First Tee – Metro Atlanta*

"This book combines in a remarkable way all you need to know about this life-changing game of golf and the principles of leadership. It will inform, educate, and inspire! Whether you are new to golf or early in your leadership career, you will not want to put it down until you are done."

> —**Dawnet Beverley**, *executive vice president of global capital markets, Donnelley Financial Solutions*

"Anna and Eric's innovative approach for addressing the needs of young people through the sport of golf can be applied by companies looking to truly make an impact in diversity, equity, and inclusion."

> —**Julie Kae**, *vice president of sustainability and DEI, executive director, Qlik.org*

"An excellent opportunity for women in STEM to learn more about leadership principles while gaining a skill they can use for personal enjoyment or professional development. This book makes sharing the model with everyone possible!"

> —**Dr. Melissa Dagley**, *executive director, Initiatives in STEM (iSTEM), University of Central Florida*

"Building meaningful relationships through the game of golf is multi-dimensional and will test your social and emotional intelligence skills. *FairWays to Leadership*® provides valuable insight into naturally occurring opportunities to build relationships while playing golf and can help you better understand how best to respond."

—**Macey Russell**, *complex trial and litigation partner, Choate, Hall & Stewart LLP*

"Succinct, immersive, and relatable. By encouraging curiosity, integrity, strategy, and mindfulness, the reader will gain valuable career advancement insights. As a leadership development professional and golf industry expert with more than thirty years of experience, I praise the efforts of the FairWays to Leadership® team for their timely commitment in support of young leaders. This book goes a long way in changing the face of leadership through the infinite power of golf."

—**Anthony G. Stepney**, *PGA Master Professional, player development*

"The essential handbook for current and future golfers to maximize their time spent on the links. From golfing basics that make the game approachable for everyone, to golfing etiquette and play tips, to practical strategies for building trust and leadership skills on the course, *FairWays to Leadership*® is an indispensable guide for those looking to strengthen their mind, character, and business with golf."

—**James P. Wisdom**, *founder and chief marketing officer, CW Strategic Marketing, and executive coach*

"The Boyds have written the book I wish I'd had decades ago. Not only would I have started playing golf ten years earlier, but I would also have enjoyed both my work and my golfing more. I wish I could get this book into the hands of every young woman aspiring to a leadership position."

—**Benita Fortner**, *retired director of supplier diversity, Raytheon Technologies*

FairWays
— to —
Leadership®

FairWays
— to —
Leadership®

Building Your Business Network
One Round of Golf at a Time

ERIC BOYD AND
ANNA ALVAREZ BOYD

Georgetown University Press / Washington, DC

The publisher is not responsible for third-party websites or their content. URL links were active at time of publication.

Library of Congress Cataloging-in-Publication Data

Names: Boyd, Eric, author. | Boyd, Anna Alvarez, author.
Title: FairWays to leadership® : building your business network one round of golf at a time / Eric Boyd and Anna Alvarez Boyd.
Description: Washington, DC : Georgetown University Press, 2024. | Includes bibliographical references and index.
Identifiers: LCCN 2022061496 (print) | LCCN 2022061497 (ebook) | ISBN 9781647123888 (paperback) | ISBN 9781647123895 (ebook)
Subjects: LCSH: Leadership. | Business networks. | Golf.
Classification: LCC HD57.7 .B689 2024 (print) | LCC HD57.7 (ebook) | DDC 658.4/092—dc23/eng/20230920
LC record available at https://lccn.loc.gov/2022061496
LC ebook record available at https://lccn.loc.gov/2022061497

♾ This paper meets the requirements of ANSI/NISO Z39.48-1992 (Permanence of Paper).

25 24   9 8 7 6 5 4 3 2   First printing

Printed in the United States of America

Cover design by Molly von Borstel, Faceout Studio
Interior design by Robert Kern, TIPS Publishing Services, Carrboro, NC

Contents

Introduction

Leadership and the Game of Golf

G olf supports leadership development by providing an environment where an individual faces many of the same challenges that are faced by leaders in their position of authority and responsibility for an organization. Sports are recognized for creating effective learning environments because they support active learning and provide immediate feedback to the learner.[1] Golf offers a unique opportunity for leadership development because it is one of the few sports where you compete primarily against yourself and the environment, opening the opportunity for the richness of self-reflection that is crucial to leadership development.[2]

It also challenges an individual in many important aspects of leadership, including integrity, adaptability, and mindfulness. Through recognizing and mastering these challenges, an individual can develop as an effective leader. The opportunities golf provides for leadership development are born out in research indicating that 85 percent of executives believe that playing golf impacts the way they act as leaders and that it is a key contributor to the quality of their leadership.[3]

Not insignificantly, golf—again, unlike most other sports—serves a prominent role in the social life of business. Ninety percent of *Fortune* 500 CEOs play golf, and of these, 80 percent play to build their professional networks while 93 percent believe it helps them develop closer relationships with individuals in their professional networks.[4] Thus, playing golf provides a unique opportunity for networking and building relationships with individuals who have influence over who can access leadership roles. These individuals can be referred to as "special playing partners," and building relationships with them is important because it is current business leaders who make decisions about the hiring and promotion of future business leaders. The popularity of golf with business leadership means that the game provides an avenue for gaining access to special playing partners who can help in acquiring leadership positions.

Charity golf events provide an excellent example of the intersection between the social life of business and golf. There are over eight hundred thousand charity golf events a year, and the vast majority are supported by businesses.[5] Support of charity events often involves personnel from a company playing in the event along with current or potential clients. Playing in your company's group provides the chance for you to spend time with individuals from your own company and with the personnel from your client. Each of them can play an influential role in your leadership journey both now and in the future.

However, the significant benefits that access to the game of golf provides haven't been within reach of everyone in the workforce. You do not have to look far to find evidence of the limited access women and people of color have to business leadership in the United States. Women make up 47 percent of the American workforce but only 5 percent of *Fortune* 500 CEOs,[6] a number that is trending down since reaching a peak of 6 percent in 2017.[7] The numbers get even starker when considering people of color. Only 3.2 percent of senior leadership roles at large companies in the United States are held by Black individuals,[8] and similarly low numbers describe the percentage of Latinx (4.3 percent) and Asian (6.9 percent) leaders in executive roles within American firms.[9] The numbers do not improve

In 2004, I left my role as a senior leader in the federal government to join Fannie Mae Corporation. Just two weeks into the new job, my boss stopped by my office with the news that I would be playing in the women's golf outing later that month. Imagine my surprise and rising panic. Golf isn't commonly used for networking in the federal government, so it was completely uncharted territory. In a leap of faith, I borrowed clubs from a neighbor who was about my height and went off to the event in complete terror. Upon arriving at Landsdowne Golf Club in Virginia, I was greeted by some colleagues and a small team of supportive women golf professionals. With patient guidance, they helped me find some straight putts and the beginning outline of what would become a decent enough swing. That day led to many happy hours on the course with my colleagues, business associates, and most importantly my family and friends. In addition, I now have access to a game I can turn to throughout my life for health and wellness.

—Anna

when you combine gender and race. Only 4.7 percent of business leadership positions in S&P 500 companies are held by women of color.[10] (As used in this book, the term "people of color" refers to underrepresented groups in business and leadership, including Black, Latinx, Asian, and Native or Indigenous people.)

The golf industry reflects the business profile described here. Of the thirty thousand golf professionals registered with the Professional Golfers' Association (PGA) of America, only 10 percent are women, and fewer than 1 percent are African Americans. Only 23 percent of all golfers are women, and only 18 percent of golfers are people of color.[11]

Several factors create barriers for new golfers to learn, play, and use golf for advancing their career. One barrier is social exclusion. Golf club rules at private clubs can limit access to women and people of color.[12] For example, Augusta National, a private golf club and home of the Masters men's golf championship played in Augusta, Georgia, only admitted its first female member in 2012, and Muirfield Golf Club, a private golf club in the United Kingdom that regularly hosts The Open men's golf championship, only began admitting female members in 2019. Public courses offer a more accessible option than private clubs because there are fewer rules associated with who can play and the cost tends to be much lower. However, public courses are less frequently patroned by special playing partners, so while public courses provide more accessibility, they do not solve inclusion issues.

Social exclusion also occurs in a less formal manner. Women can be made to feel unwelcome when golf courses, both private and public, make efforts to accommodate men but not women.[13] One place where this can happen is in the pro shop. Women feel unwanted when they go into the pro shop and see only a smattering of merchandise catered to them but a room full of men's shirts, shoes, hats, and related clothing and golf accessories. A lack of female staff or staff of color also creates a sense of social exclusion, as do event calendars full of golf outings for men but only a single day for women's events. A visit to the pro shop or website will provide insight into the extent to which women are welcome and accommodated at a course.

In addition to aspects of the golf course being a social barrier, perceptions of women and people of color can also play a role in making the game feel unwelcoming.[14] These perceptions are communicated in statements made in frustration on the golf course, like a male golfer saying "Hit it, Alice" when his putt comes up short. They are also communicated in microaggressions that occur when red tee markers are described as "the ladies' tees," which limits the options of women golfers to one set of tee markers while men can choose from any of the tee markers on a tee box. These perceptions and the statements they motivate can make the game uninviting and reduce the likelihood of participation by women. Furthermore, racial stereotypes related to sports intelligence can both shape how people of color are treated and negatively impact their ability to play well.[15]

Regardless of race and gender, golf presents economic challenges for many new players. Golf is not a cheap sport. Playing requires buying a set of clubs, a golf bag, balls, and tees. Collared shirts and other clothing necessary to meet dress code requirements add to the cost. Furthermore, green fees must be paid each time you play. Improving at the game requires spending time (and money) at the driving range, and hiring a golf coach can cost seventy-five to one hundred dollars for an hour-long lesson.[16]

In addition to the social and economic barriers, special challenges also arise when using golf to access leaders and leadership opportunities. First, playing a round of golf can take a considerable amount of time, ranging from four to five hours depending on the pace of play. As a result, golf provides a longer period of access to leaders compared with other avenues of access like meetings or dinners. You must plan for the length of this engagement but remain flexible to react as events unfold during the round.

A second unique challenge is the informal nature of the time you will spend with your special playing partner. The golfing experience takes place away from the office and outside in nature. This leads to more informal interactions, where topics range from business to personal. You must remember this difference while taking advantage of the opportunity informality provides for developing rapport with a special playing partner.

Third, special playing partners are business leaders who might often use a round of golf to evaluate potential leaders, inside or outside their organizations, whom they are considering as business partners. For example, Jack Welch, former CEO of GE, routinely played golf with potential executives because he believed the time, informality, and nature of golf provided unique insight into the leadership character of a person.[17] Thus, acting in ways that positively reflect you as a leader is important.

Navigating the Challenges

What can be done to overcome the challenges? This book outlines how the game of golf provides valuable lessons in leadership to help underrepresented individuals in the business world. Challenges occur at multiple points during a golfing experience. As a result, playing a round of golf involves many moments where leadership skills are required, hereafter referred to as "leadership moments" on the course.

The first leadership moment occurs at the clubhouse. Being a leader at this moment requires identifying special playing partners whom you can network with on the golf course. This requires planning the round, making the invite, and preparing your special playing partner for the golf outing. The next leadership moment occurs at the practice area. Spending time at the putting green and driving range before starting the round ensures your mind and body are ready for playing and engaging with your special playing partner. The next leadership moment occurs at the tee box. The tee box represents one of the few times at each hole where you and your special playing partner come together and hit from the same spot on the course, which provides an opportunity for engaging with your special playing partner and developing a relationship with them. There are also leadership moments in the fairway and at the green, each of which allows you an opportunity to best leverage your networking during the round. After the round, a leadership moment occurs at the nineteenth hole, when you host the playing partner in the clubhouse and have a chance to discuss opportunities with them. Here is where the actions taken and the decisions you've made at each of the prior leadership moments combine to determine your business success with the round.

How can you successfully navigate these different leadership moments? In the next chapter, we describe the skills and behaviors needed on the course and in the business environment. These include acting in ways that reflect curiosity, adaptability, empowerment, integrity, mindfulness, and strategy. Employing these behaviors will provide you with an opportunity to display your business leadership ability because these six behaviors are often associated with being an effective leader. Thus, learning these six leadership behaviors and deploying them during a round of golf will position you to most benefit from time on the golf course with business leaders.

Golf Like a Leader

As you play a round of golf you will experience moments when you are in the spotlight (off the tee), in trouble (in the bunker), and just where you belong (right down the fairway). Just like business challenges, how you handle these moments says something about your leadership brand. The six leadership skills described in this chapter can be practiced on the course and in the boardroom. Building an awareness of how you demonstrate these skills in different situations will help you build confidence on and off the golf course.

Curiosity

One leadership behavior required for successfully managing leadership moments that arise when using golf to access business leadership is curiosity. A curious person seeks knowledge and is open to new ways of doing things.[18] Curious people ask questions like "why," "what if," and "how could." Curious people are also good listeners because they emphasize learning from others. Curiosity is considered an important trait of business leaders because it enables leaders to effectively accomplish important business goals requiring innovation and creativity. Considering more alternatives for addressing a problem or capturing an opportunity contributes to better outcomes. Curious leaders also make fewer decision errors because they are more willing to question the status quo and think more deeply about a decision or issue facing the people they lead. Curiosity also helps to develop deeper and more trusting relationships because of the tendency of curious leaders to take the perspective of others into consideration when making decisions. As a result, people led by a curious leader are often more motivated, perform higher, and are more satisfied with their job.[19] Partly because of these benefits, 83 percent of leaders say they value and promote curiosity in their counterparts and employees.[20]

Curiosity is important when using golf to access business leadership because of the information that needs to be collected and the many decisions that must be made before, during, and after the golf round. Before the round you need to learn your playing partner's golfing abilities and interests so that proper courses and tee times can be arranged. The extended time spent playing will inevitably present many opportunities to engage in small talk with your playing partners. Asking open-ended questions during the round allows you to develop strong and trustworthy relationships. Likewise, each hole on the course is different, which will require you to look at each shot in different ways. Additionally, curiosity is also important when opportunities to discuss topics more in-depth present themselves as you share a drink or food in the clubhouse at the nineteenth hole after the round.

Adaptability

A second leadership behavior that is critical to success when using golf to access business leadership is adaptability. This leadership trait refers to one's ability to sense and respond to change.[21] Being adaptable requires a leader to be flexible in renegotiating outcomes and tapping into their intuition and negotiation skills. Adaptability is especially important in environments that change often. Through their ability to adapt, a leader can respond effectively to changes in technology, social values, politics, or economic conditions and use change as a source for competitive advantage in the marketplace. For these reasons, adaptability is one of the top five skills leaders recognize as key to success in the future.[22]

Adaptability is also important during a golfing experience with a special playing partner. Before a round, you may need to adapt to the arrival time of your special playing partner at the clubhouse. The extended time of the round will undoubtedly result in unexpected situations associated with golf shots, information shared during a round, or other causes. If the pace of play slows down significantly, you may need to switch to a best ball format. Adaptability can also be important after the round, when you may have to adapt if your special playing partner decides not to join you at the nineteenth hole. Staying open to changing circumstances will greatly enhance the experience for you and others.

Empowerment

Empowerment is another important leadership trait to rely on when using golf to access business leadership. It reflects the degree of autonomy, self-direction, and control one has over a task. When empowered, individuals feel more committed to a task, perform better in completing the task, and gain greater satisfaction from the experience.[23] Business leaders recognize the importance of empowerment for the outcomes it makes possible, but also because 70 percent of employees consider being empowered to be critical to their effective engagement within an organization.[24] Feeling fully empowered allows you to integrate your knowledge, skills, and abilities to make the best decision possible for the challenge ahead of you.

The importance of empowerment appears in many situations before, during, and after a round of golf being used to access business leadership. For example, it can play a role prior to the round when choosing a course that will allow you and your special playing partner to play your best so that playing golf does not get in the way of developing and nurturing a relationship. Likewise, empowerment is important in many instances during the round, such as when deciding which set of tee boxes to play. It can also be important after the round in the decision of whether or how to meet with your special playing partner off the course.

Integrity

Integrity is important when using golf to access business leadership. Individuals who act with integrity respect both laws and norms in a situation. The value of integrity for a leader rests on how it impacts others' expectations of how they will be treated. Individuals who see their leader acting with integrity are more likely to believe that the leader will treat them well and do what's right for an organization.[25] That's why integrity is one of the top traits both leaders and employees value in an individual.[26] Individuals display their integrity when they clearly communicate their values and act in alignment with those values.[27]

While using golf to access business leadership, an individual faces many situations before, during, and after the round that require integrity for success in developing and nurturing relationships with their special playing partners. Simple acts like checking in an appropriate amount of time before the round begins, following playing norms during the round, and correctly reporting your score after the round all require integrity and will signal your values to your special playing partner. Failure to act with integrity during any point of the golfing experience can cause your special playing partner to question your character, limiting your success in forming a relationship with them.

Mindfulness

Mindfulness refers to where you place your attention. When people are being more mindful, they focus on noticing what is happening around them in the present rather than rehearsing some future event or replaying some past event.[28] Mindfulness offers many benefits to business leaders. It is associated with being more creative, recognizing and leveraging opportunities as they emerge, and being viewed as more likeable and charismatic.[29]

Being mindful is critical to success in using golf to access business leadership. For example, before the round you need to be mindful to treat your playing partner as a guest. Mindfulness is also important during the round. You need to stay mindful, for instance, by not letting your attention stray to your score but instead remaining focused on developing and nurturing your relationship with your playing partner. Mindfulness is also important after the round when you are trying to ensure your objective for the round is achieved.

Strategy

Lastly, you need to act strategically when using golf for the purpose of accessing business leadership. For business leaders, strategy involves analyzing a situation, planning to achieve an objective, and undertaking the actions required to implement the plan.[30] Given the importance of strategy in effective leadership, many firms have begun to formally incorporate strategy into decision-making by creating the position of chief strategy officer.[31]

Strategy is important before, during, and after the golf experience being used to access business leadership. A great deal of planning takes place before the round. These plans are implemented during and after the round, all with the intention of developing and nurturing a relationship with business leadership.

By incorporating the six leadership traits, you will be more successful in developing and nurturing relationships with leadership during your golfing experience. You will also be able to demonstrate your leadership abilities to your special playing partners who may be in positions to offer you leadership and business opportunities. Now that we have reviewed the six leadership behaviors, it is time to discuss specifically how they come into play before the round, when you are heading to the clubhouse and the driving range. Equally important is how the six leadership behaviors contribute during the round, when you head to the tee box, the fairway, and the green. Last, the leadership behaviors also play important roles after the round, when you head to the nineteenth hole and then back to the office.

It's time to provide the important details. Let's head to the clubhouse and see what decisions and actions are required to use golf for accessing business leadership and how you can use the six leadership behaviors to effectively move through leadership moments in the golfing experience.

Golf 101

The use of golf in business requires preparation ranging from having the right equipment to practicing how to swing the club to knowing the rules and etiquette of the game. These are some of the basics that are important to know for you to play effectively on the golf course and use golf in your professional career. Being able to successfully navigate the golf journey from the clubhouse all the way back to the workplace is also required, but you must be able to play before the journey can begin. In this chapter, you'll learn the basics you need to know to start playing golf.

Designated Areas and Rules

The United States Golf Association (USGA) is the governing body for golf in the United States and Mexico while the Royal and Ancient Golf Club (R&A) is the governing body for all other areas in the world. These organizations cooperate in setting rules pertaining to the five designated areas of a golf course: the teeing area, penalty areas, bunkers, the putting green, and the general area.

On each golf hole, play begins in the teeing area. A player can set the ball on a tee or place the ball on the ground to hit it and begin play on a hole. One of the more important rules for the teeing area specifies where you can hit the ball in the tee box. Each tee box has multiple sets of tee markers that differ by color. At the beginning of a round of golf, a player chooses which set of tee markers they will play for the round (e.g., blue markers). The player must then tee the ball up between the two tee markers of their chosen set on each hole. For example, if you choose to play the blue tee markers, you must tee your ball up between the two blue tee marks on the tee box. You cannot tee the ball up outside of the blue tee markers, and you can't line your ball up in front of the two markers. The only flexibility you have is that you can go back two club lengths from the blue tee markers to tee up the ball, but the tee must stay within the markers.

The golf course also has many penalty areas that we will cover in more detail throughout the book. The more commonly experienced hazards involve water hazards and out-of-bounds markers. Any body of water on a golf course is a potential water hazard, including ponds, lakes, ditches, rivers, or other open water areas. Water hazards are marked by either red or yellow stakes. According to the USGA, if your ball falls into a yellow water hazard, you can drop your ball behind the water in taking relief to continue playing. There is a penalty stroke assessed for doing so. A red stake marks water hazards where it is not possible to take relief by dropping a ball behind the hazard. In this case, you drop the ball by bending down and releasing it from knee height. If it keeps rolling back to the hazard after three tries, you can instead place it on the ground. There is a one-stroke penalty for taking relief from a red water hazard. The other common hazard is out-of-bounds areas, which are marked by white stakes on the perimeter of a hole. The penalty for hitting a ball out of bounds is one stroke, and you must rehit a ball from where you hit the shot that went out of bounds. Often, going out of bounds is described as a stroke-and-distance hazard because you must add strokes to your score and lose the distance you hit the ball that went out of bounds. Alternatively, water hazards involve only a stroke penalty.

The bunkers of a golf course are depressions in the ground that are often manmade and created to test a player's ability to hit the ball from sand. Bunkers located around the green are called traps or green-side bunkers. Bunkers in the fairway area between the tee box and green are often called fairway bunkers. One of the more infamous types of bunkers is a pot bunker, which is round and has vertical walls that make it hard to advance the ball forward if you go into one. The main rule to remember if you go into a bunker is that you cannot let your club touch the sand before you make your swing to hit the ball. It's referred to as "grounding" your club if it happens, and you are assessed a one-stroke penalty.

The next designated area is the green, which is located at the end of each golf hole and contains the hole. (We know the word "hole" is used to describe both one of the units of play on a golf course and the hole on the green at the end of a unit of play. Knowing which one someone is talking about is situational and something you learn from experience playing the game.) The green is the only place on the course where you can physically touch the ball once it is in play. Otherwise, you must play the ball as it lies, except to take a drop from a hazard as discussed earlier. On the green, you are allowed to do things that you can't do on other parts of the golf hole, such as marking, lifting, and cleaning your ball; repairing damage to the green; and removing sand and loose soil. One of the important rules on the green is that you can't "test" the green, meaning you can't roll a ball to see how fast or in which direction your putt may move. Also, if you are in someone's line of play, you can move your mark over with your putter head, but you must remember to put it back in its original spot. If you do not, you receive a one-stroke penalty. A recent rule change on the green has to do with the flag. Until recently, you were penalized if you putted the ball on the green and it struck the flagstick while in the hole. That rule was eliminated, and you can now putt with the flag in or out of the hole.

The last designated area of the golf course is the general area. The general area encompasses everywhere on the course except the teeing area, the hazards, the green, and bunkers. For example, the fairway, representing the part of the hole between the tee box and green, is considered a general area, along with the woods and the tall grassy areas (called "rough") surrounding the fairway.

Clubs and Balls

One area of preparation involves having the right equipment. The main types of clubs you will need are woods, irons, wedges, and a putter. The rules of golf allow you to carry a maximum of fourteen clubs with you during a round. A typical set of golf clubs will include three woods (driver and two fairway woods), seven irons (3, 4, 5, 6, 7, 8, and 9 irons), three wedges (52, 56, and 60 degrees), and a putter. The woods are often used to hit from the tee box when you can put the ball on a tee to hit your drive to start play on a hole. Golfers also hit their woods in the fairway when they have a long distance to carry, with the exception being the driver, which is most often only used on the tee box. In the end, it should be mentioned that club selection all depends on each player. People can play the same club yet hit different distances and trajectories, which is why practicing on the driving range and learning how far you hit with each club is key.

Most often, the irons are used from the fairway when hitting approach shots to the green. You can also hit from the tee box with your irons, especially on shorter holes like par 3s. The par on a hole represents the number of golf strokes an average golfer is expected to require to get the ball into the hole from the tee box on a golf hole. A course is generally made up of a combination of par 3, par

4, and par 5 holes. The expectation when determining the par score (3, 4, or 5) for a hole of golf is that it takes two putts on the green to get the ball in the hole. Thus, for a par 4 hole, a player is expected to take one stroke to hit the ball from the tee box (the area where the play for a hole begins) into the fairway (the landing area for a ball hit straight from the tee box), one stroke to hit the ball from the fairway onto the green (the area containing the golf hole), and two strokes to putt the ball into the hole on the green. The wedges are used to hit the ball onto the green when a player is close to the hole (usually 100 yards and closer), and the putter is used to putt the ball into the hole.

Clubs differ in the length of the shaft connecting the handle to the club head and the angle, or lie, of the club head relative to the ground. The length of the shaft is longer for the lower numbered clubs and shorter for the higher numbered clubs. What does this all mean for the game of golf? Generally, a longer shaft allows you to hit the ball farther. This is good when you want distance, which is why most people use lower numbered clubs (e.g., 4 iron) when they have a longer distance for the ball to travel to the green. Conversely, most players use a higher numbered club (e.g., 9 iron) for a shorter distance.

The angle of the club face also varies. The angle is less on lower numbered clubs, meaning the club face is more upright. The flatter club face combined with the longer shaft is why you can hit the golf ball further with lowered number clubs. Alternatively, the club face is more open with higher numbered clubs, allowing you to hit the ball short but high when combined with the shorter shaft. You want to take advantage of the higher ball flight when close to the hole so that the ball will stop on the green. The putter generally has the shortest shaft and the flattest face. The flat face of the putter allows you to roll the ball on the green toward the hole.

You aren't required to have fourteen clubs in your golf bag, but make sure you don't have more than that in your bag when you start a round. What happens if you do have more than fourteen clubs in your bag when you begin the round? The rules of golf require that you take a two-stroke penalty, meaning that two strokes are added to your score on the hole you played carrying more than fourteen clubs. You may wonder how you can end up with extra clubs in your bag. It's easy. Just ask Ian Woosnam about his experience at the 2001 Open Championship played at Royal Lytham & St Annes Golf Club in Lytham St Annes, England. The Open Championship is a tournament for male golfers held annually in the United Kingdom. It is considered one of the major men's golf championships because it is the oldest golf tournament and typically has the strongest field of international golfing professionals playing in the tournament.

In the 2001 Open Championship, Ian Woosnam entered the final day of the tournament as a coleader. On the second hole tee box, he realized that he had fifteen clubs in his bag and told tournament officials, who advised him that he would have to take a two-stroke penalty and add the strokes to his score on the first hole. How did he end up with fifteen clubs in his bag? He had been hitting two drivers during practice and had decided on one of them for his round. The problem was that the second driver was never removed from his bag in the time between practicing and playing the first hole. The easy way to make sure that you don't have too many clubs in your bag is to simply take a count of your clubs before starting each round. It will save you strokes and keep you from the embarrassment of a simple but costly golfing mistake.

Events at major golf tournaments like what happened to Ian Woosnam at the 2001 Open Championship are often the subject of discussion between golfers. Thus, it is important for you to follow what happens in these tournaments so you can engage in golfing conversations and show your knowledge of the game to others. The Open Championship is not the only major men's golf tournament. There are three other men's major golf tournaments: the US Men's Open, the PGA Championship, and the Masters Golf Tournament. Major golf tournaments for women include the ANA Inspiration, the US Women's Open, the Women's PGA Championship, the Evian Championship, and the Women's British Open. These tournaments are typically televised, so be sure to catch some if not all of them when they're played so that you can participate in golf-related discussions at work and on the course.

It's perfectly acceptable to start golfing with a used set of golf clubs. One reason is that you are just learning the golf swing and your swing will adjust over time as you learn more about the proper techniques and improve. A second reason for starting with a set of used clubs is that it keeps your start-up costs low and frees up money for you to spend more time practicing and playing. There are a couple of things to look for when considering a used set of clubs. You want the grips of the clubs to be in good shape. Very worn, thin, tattered grips will have to be replaced, and that will cost you between seventy and one hundred dollars, depending on which grips you choose to install. It is also important that all clubs in the used set are from the same brand and manufacturer. Golf clubs are like cars in that manufacturers offer different brands of golf clubs and introduce new designs yearly, just like car manufacturers sell multiple car brands and introduce new designs yearly. You want a set from the same brand because you will get more consistent ball flight from each club, and this will help in your development and playing as a golfer. Lastly, it's important to find a set of clubs that fit your height and swing.

When you're looking for your first set of clubs, look for a starter set that is made for beginners. These clubs are designed to be more forgiving when you hit the ball with them. Be sure to stay away from the cheapest clubs that are likely to be the lowest quality. Good quality clubs allow for more adjustments to be made to the club if you decide after buying them that you need a different length for the shaft, which is the straight and rounded piece of metal to which the club face is attached in forming a golf club. You are usually safe from a quality perspective if you buy one of the well-known golf brands, like Callaway, Titleist, Ping, and TaylorMade.

You always want to swing the clubs before you buy them. Notice if they feel too heavy or too light when you swing. Also, do you feel comfortable with the look of the clubface when you put it behind the ball as you prepare to swing and strike the ball? Golf club manufacturers vary significantly in how they design the clubface. Some are small while others are larger. Some are thicker while others are thinner. You want to feel confident on the course, and being comfortable with the look of the club is important. It is also important when you're considering a new set of clubs to determine if it is a boxed set or regular set. A boxed set will come with everything you need to play a round of golf, including a set of irons, a golf bag to carry them, a putter, wedges, and woods. However, a regular set typically only includes irons, and you will need to buy the golf bag and other clubs like the putter and driver separately.

There are golf clubs designed specifically for men and women. However, don't buy based on gender. In other words, don't let someone look at you and recommend you buy a set based on your gender. The best approach is to buy the set of clubs you feel most comfortable swinging and which fit your swing. That means it is advisable to get a club fitting. Most stores that sell clubs will offer a service to identify the best type of clubs for you based on an analysis of your swing. This can be very beneficial and help you get the most yardage and accuracy from your clubs.

You will also need golf balls to play each hole. We say "golf balls," plural, because it is inevitable that at some point in every round you will either have to replace a lost ball or want to switch out your ball because it has gotten scuffed or marked in some way that doesn't make it unplayable but could negatively affect the flight of the ball. Therefore, it's always good practice to have several balls in your bag when you start a round. All golf balls are the same size, as stipulated by the governing bodies of the game that are responsible for setting the rules for play and equipment used in the game.

While the rules of golf stipulate the size of a golf ball, there are differences in how the balls are constructed, which should be taken into consideration when choosing a golf ball. Golf balls are made with either a surlyn ionomer or a urethane cover, within which sits a hard rubber core. What does this mean when choosing a golf ball? A surlyn cover is harder than a urethane cover, which allows it to be more resistant to damage and last longer. However, the hard surface of the surlyn cover makes it more difficult to control when you hit it. There is also a price difference. Surlyn-covered balls are typically priced lower than urethane-covered balls.

Golf balls also differ in the number of layers used to construct them. Two layers is the minimum number used to make a golf ball, but the layers can get as many as five. The hardest layer is generally the inner layer closest to the core, and the layers get less hard closer to the cover of the ball. What impact does the number of layers have on ball flight? Typically, you can expect more control with more layers and more distance with fewer layers.

Are you starting to see a trend when it comes to these specifications? You can go for more distance or more control, but it's hard to get both. With beginning players, it's best to opt for distance until you start to regularly hit the ball a good distance and can focus more on control. What is a "good distance" for the average player? Data gathered by *Golf Digest*, a leading golf publication, suggest the following as approximate median distances for the average player: driver (220 yards), 7-iron (133 yards), and pitching wedge (74 yards).[1] Stay with a surlyn-covered ball with fewer layers until you start to hit these distances with your clubs.

Golf Accessories

There are also several accessory pieces of equipment that aren't required but are good to have in your bag. The first of these is tees that you can use to tee up the ball on the tee boxes beginning play on each hole. A tee is not required to hit from the tee box. In fact, early golfers simply made little mounds of dirt to tee the ball up, and the rules still allow you to do this. However, the cost of tees is not great, and you get a lot less dirty using tees, so use one if possible. Tees come in various sizes, colors, and materials. It's pretty much a personal choice, so feel free to express yourself with your tee selection.

Another piece of accessory equipment is a ball marker. Once you hit the ball on the tee box and it's in play, the rules of golf do not allow you to touch the ball, except with the club when making a swing, until the ball is on the green. You can use a marker to mark the ball's position on the green. To mark the ball, approach the ball from behind the line you plan to putt toward the hole and place the marker in the ground as close as possible to the ball without touching it. You can then pick up the ball and clean it before replacing it to hit your putt. To replace the ball, approach the mark from the same direction and put the ball down just in front of the marker. Then, you can remove the marker and proceed to putt the ball. Markers are most often round and should have some weight to them so they don't move in the wind. You can buy a marker or use any object you have that is about the size and weight of a quarter.

A divot repair tool is also an important piece of accessory equipment to have in your bag. It is used to repair indentations (referred to as "divots") that your ball makes on the green when it lands hard enough to leave a mark. Repairing your divots is not a rule, but part of the etiquette of golf includes the expectation to leave the course, including the green, in as good a shape as you found it, if not better. How can you make it better? Many times, you may find that others do not follow golf etiquette and repair their divots or the marks made by their shoes when walking on the green. In those cases, you have the opportunity to repair those divots and leave the course better than you found it. This is also a very easy and effective way to demonstrate your understanding and appreciation of the game to your special playing partner. Divot repair tools can be a separate piece of equipment, or they can be combined with a ball marker.

Most players also carry a towel and use it in several ways, such as drying their hands on a hot day. This is very important, as I found out once when play-ing with a set of clubs I had rented from the pro shop. (Most pro shops will have sets of clubs you can rent if you don't have your clubs with you for some reason.) It was so hot that there were very few people on the course. As a result, I ended up playing alone. The sixth hole at that course is a 115 yard par 3 with a small pond between the tee box and green that must be hit over from the tee box. I grabbed a wedge from my golf bag on this hot day and proceeded to take aim at the flag on the green and make a swing. During the swing and right after I struck the ball, the club slipped out of my grip and flew into the air just behind the ball until it got about midway over the pond. At that point, gravity took over, and the wedge fell into the pond and sank to the bottom. I played the rest of the round without a wedge and had to pay seventy-five dollars in the pro shop to replace the club. All of this may not have happened if I had just used a towel to wipe my hands before making the swing.

Having a towel is also handy to clean your clubs after striking the ball. This occurs most often with the irons because they can pick up dirt when striking the ball as it sits in the fairway or in the rough. Your club may also need cleaning after you hit out of a sand trap to remove sand from the clubface. Towels come in various sizes and colors and often include wording. Like the other pieces of accessory equipment, the choice of a towel is an opportunity to express some-thing about yourself to your special playing partners and create a topic of con-versation in the process.

Lastly, it is strongly recommended that you include sunscreen lotion or spray and a hat in your bag to prevent sunburn. Golf is an outdoor activity that exposes you to the sun for an extended amount of time. You will get sunburn if you are not careful, and some of the best ways to protect against the sun are to wear a hat and apply sun protection to your skin.

Golf Attire

The R&A and USGA do not have rules regulating what you can and cannot wear to play golf. Golf courses, however, often do have dress codes for players and it's always good to call ahead to a course you plan to play and ask. In general, golf shoes, a collared shirt, and some form of pants, skirt, or golf dress are required to play. Shoes will typically have cleats on the bottom to help you maintain your stance when swinging the club. These cleats should be rubber but are not required on all shoes. The traditional style of golf shoe that has been accepted is a loafer design, but that is changing, and now you can find golf shoes in a tennis shoe design. The choice of shoe should be made based on comfort because you will be doing a lot of walking and want to make sure you are comfortable during the round.

Most golf courses require golfers to wear a collared shirt. Traditionally, this meant a raised collar, but more and more courses are accepting shirts with flat collars. Golf shirts have short sleeves in most cases. Yet, an increasing number of players wear long-sleeve t-shirts underneath their golf shirt as an additional layer of protection from the sun or for added warmth during the winter months. Sweaters and rain jackets are also acceptable forms of clothing to cover your upper body for warmth and protection against the elements.

Acceptable attire for your lower body includes slacks but not jeans. Women often wear skirts or golf dresses; just make sure they are an adequate length for the course you are playing. Wearing shorts is a bit trickier because there is not a consensus on the topic among golfers. Many golf clubs, especially upscale private ones, frown upon and may prohibit the wearing of shorts. As always, it's a good idea to call ahead and ask before playing a new course or, at least, wear nice shorts that are longer in length and free of wear and tear.

It's important to pause here and point out that the clothes you wear are meant to ensure you meet the dress code for the course you are playing and to allow you to express yourself. The clothes you wear will not make you play better, but others will form an impression of you based on what you wear. For example, Jesse Penn, a Howard University engineering graduate and friend, described a situation early in his professional career when he had just been hired away from IBM by Johnson & Johnson.[2] Three weeks after arriving, he was told to prepare to play in the annual company golf tournament in the upcoming month. Never having played golf before, Jesse bought the required equipment and the optional accessory equipment. After taking a few lessons, he showed up for the company tournament only to find that he had been paired to play with the president of the company. Jesse felt nervous, as one might expect when about to spend the next four hours playing an unfamiliar game with someone holding influence over your professional future. Jesse became even more nervous when the president arrived and was decked out with expensive leather golf shoes and the latest golf fashion. If the president's clothes matched his play, it was about to be a long day for Jesse. However, the clothes couldn't help the president as he proceeded to hit his drive on the first hole only 50 yards and it didn't get much better from there. The point of this story is to dress for comfort, dress to express yourself, and dress to accommodate the dress codes at the course you're playing.

Golf Swing

You'll need to be able to swing the golf club so that you can play the game. You don't need to be a great golfer to play. According to research by the National Golf Foundation, 66 percent of golfers score more than 90 for a round of golf.[3] For comparison, par for most courses is 72, meaning that most golfers take an extra 18 strokes or more to get the ball into the hole during a round of golf. This means that great playing is not required to play a round of golf. What's most important is that your pace of play is good. Pace of play refers to how quickly or slowly you play a hole and round of golf. Playing at a faster rather than slower pace is most preferable. In fact, many people care much less about how well you play and much more about whether you maintain a good pace of play because no one wants to spend five hours or more on the golf course. We'll talk more about pace of play when we discuss the leadership moments associated with golf.

Many people take golf lessons to help them swing the club better, and it is highly recommended that you do so. Golf teaching is a $1 billion industry. You will want to find a certified golf instructor because they have been trained in teaching golf and are expert golfers themselves and can draw on both their training and experience to help you learn to swing the club effectively. Two organizations that certify golf teachers are the PGA of America and the Ladies Professional Golf Association (LPGA). A search online using the phrase "PGA golf instructor" or "LPGA golf instructor" will typically identify many individuals in your area whom you can contact about receiving golf lessons.

You'll want to learn how to hit different types of clubs and shots. Tiger Woods, who many believe is the greatest golfer of all time, describes in *How I Play Golf* that he started learning to play golf by putting.[4] Starting with putting is good because it's easy to learn and is a quick way to start building your confidence with golf. Starting with putting is also a good way to practice the shots that you are going to hit the most. To prove this, let's do a little math. A golf course typically has 18 holes. If par for a round is 72 strokes for the 18 holes, then it means that 36 (2 putts per hole) is the expected number of putts in a round. That's 50 percent of the strokes (36/72) in a par round. No other club accounts for as much of a player's score as the putter, so starting to learn how to play golf by learning how to putt is just smart golf.

A good next step is to learn how to pitch and chip the ball onto the green. Both types of shots are hit when your ball lies close to but not on the green. A pitch shot flies higher and stops shortly after landing on the green. A chip shot flies lower and rolls more once it lands on the green. The pitch shot and chip shot are both important to help your scoring because they determine how long or short of a putt you have on the green. Together, putting, pitching, and chipping make up what is referred to as the "short game" because they all involve short shots made just off (i.e., pitching and chipping) or on (i.e., putting) the green.

You'll also need to learn how to hit your irons and woods. Keep in mind that very few players ever hit a completely straight golf shot. Ben Hogan is credited with being one of the greatest ball strikers of all time. He is also known to have said, "You only hit a straight ball by accident."[5] If one of the greatest golfers of all time doesn't expect to hit straight, then you shouldn't either. Rather, what is important is to be consistent hitting the ball so that it flies the same way as often as possible. If you do that, then you can play for the shot and play much better. The types of shots you might hit are described by the flight of the ball. A ball that only slightly flies from right to left is called a "draw" while a ball that flies a great deal from right to left is called a "hook." However, a ball that only slightly flies from left to right is called a "fade" while a ball that flies a great deal from left to right is called a "slice." A good teacher will help you discover your typical ball flight and work with you to get more consistent in hitting that flight.

Golf Scoring

You'll also need to know how to keep score of your golf play before you begin. Golf is a game with its own language, and scoring is no different. Often, golfers describe their score on a hole not by the number of strokes it took them to get the ball into the hole but by the terms given to certain scores. We've already used the term "par" to describe the score for a golfer who gets the ball into the hole in the expected number of strokes for a golf hole. That means it takes you three strokes to get the ball into the hole on a par 3, four strokes on a par 4, and five strokes on a par 5. How do you know what par is for a golf hole? You can find this information in two places. One place is the scorecard for a golf course. All golf courses will provide you with a scorecard at no cost. The scorecard will list each hole and indicate the par score. The second place you can find information about the par for a hole is the tee box. Signage at the beginning of each hole will indicate that hole's par score. We'll return to the scorecard and tee box signage once we start discussing leadership moments on the course.

We've talked a lot about a par score so far. However, we also discussed how most golfers shoot much higher than par (e.g., see the earlier point about 66 percent of golfers shooting 90 or higher for a round of golf). Golf has terms for scores other than par. If you take one stroke more than par, then your score is called a "bogey." Two strokes more than par is called a "double bogey." Guess what three strokes over par is called? You guessed it, a "triple bogey." Last question related to being over par: What if you're four strokes over par on a hole? There is no term for this because most golfers know to pick up their ball and end their play on a hole if they get to a score of four strokes or higher for a hole. Doing so is not considered rude but just the opposite. It is considered good manners or etiquette to avoid taking too long on any one hole. (Golf has many rules for etiquette. We'll talk about them as we discuss the leadership moments on the golf course.) A recommendation here is to confirm what's acceptable with your playing partners before you start playing. An exception is when you are playing a round in competition. In that case, you must play the ball into the hole even if it requires four or more strokes over par.

There are also terms for when you play a golf hole very well and your score is under par. Play a hole in one fewer stroke than par, and it's called a "birdie." For example, you can tell your playing partner that you have a birdie for a par 3 if it only takes you two strokes to get the ball into the golf hole from the tee box. The term used to describe requiring two strokes fewer than par to get the ball into the hole on the green is called an "eagle," while taking three strokes fewer than par is referred to as an "albatross."

We've covered some of the basics of golf that you'll need to know before starting your use of golf to advance your professional career. You have your clubs, your accessory equipment, and your attire. You've also learned about the importance of learning to swing the club and advance the ball consistently with your swing. You also know how to score your play on each hole. It's now time to head to the golf course and learn about the leadership moments that await you at the clubhouse, practice area, tee box, fairway, green, and nineteenth hole. Let's get going.

Leadership at the Clubhouse

The clubhouse at a golf course is the main building where a golfer checks in to start their round of golf. The clubhouse also serves other functions that we'll discuss, but first it's important to note the origins of the clubhouse and its linkage with the origins of golf so that we gain a better understanding of the clubhouse's place in the game and golfing experience with your special playing partner. The first recorded game of golf was played in Scotland during the fourteenth century. At that time, the game was played along the sand dunes surrounding Edinburgh, Scotland. There weren't actual courses, but they did have sand dunes, and the players would use a stick to hit a pebble over or around sand dunes. The game became so popular that it was eventually banned by the king of England, who controlled Scotland at that time. England needed Scottish archers to be ready to defend against any attack, but the archers, and many others it seems, were so taken with the game of golf that they were playing rather than practicing their archery skills. This led the king of England to outlaw the game of golf so that archers would spend their time practicing archery rather than their golf game.

In the early seventeenth century, King James I of England lifted the ban on golf and endorsed the game, as did King James VI of Scotland. In 1744, the first golf club was formed by a group of players who shared a common enjoyment of playing golf and decided to call their golf group "The Honorable Company of Edinburgh." At this time, golf courses did not have main buildings, only a golf club in a social sense of members who all played the same course. Thus, before there was a building we would call a clubhouse, there was a social group of golfers called the golf club. In 1768, The Honorable Company decided it would be nice if they had an actual place where they could meet and built the first clubhouse. Thus, the clubhouse grew out of the social nature of the game as people playing the same golf course wanted a place where they could meet before and after playing a round of golf. Keeping that in mind will help you understand the role of the clubhouse. It really is the social place on the golf course where people meet and spend time before and after their golfing experience.

Today's clubhouses vary. Saint Andrews Golf Course in St. Andrews, Scotland, is considered the oldest golf course; it has a very grand clubhouse. Other clubhouses are much less grand, having a more minimalist appearance. The point is that you're going to see clubhouses that vary in size and design, but they all play a very similar role to serve as the place where people come to start their round, gather to talk about their golf experience, and spend time together after a round of golf.

While their design will vary, you can expect a clubhouse to consist of three primary areas: the pro shop, the food and beverage area, and the locker rooms. The pro shop is the retail area of the clubhouse because it is where you make your tee time and pay for your round prior to starting. The pro shop also sells merchandise such as golf clubs, bags, and balls. You can also buy golf clothes in the clubhouse. There will be a counter in the pro shop where you'll find the staff. Often, the pro shop attendant is a golf professional who has undergone extensive training in golf coaching, merchandising, custom fitting, sport science, and golf management.[1] When golfers arrive and are ready to play their round, they will check in at the pro shop and the attendant will make sure all the players are there and take payment for the green fee from everyone in the group. The pro shop also sells range balls to practice with before your round.

The pro shop is traditionally where you would set your tee time by either calling on the phone or going in person. We say "traditionally" because there are an increasing number of golf apps available that allow you to set a tee time online without speaking to anyone in the pro shop. Regardless of whether you do it in person, over the phone, or online using an app, you'll need to indicate when you would like to play and how many are in your group. The maximum number of players allowed in a group is four. If you have more than four players, you will need to set two tee times or more depending upon how many people are in your group. To figure out the number of tee times you'll need, just divide the number of players by four. Now, in situations where you don't have four players for your group, you can still make a tee time, but the pro shop may add other players to your group to create a foursome. Thus, your twosome may end up playing as a foursome with two other people you don't know.

It's always advisable to create a foursome when you're setting up a golfing experience with a special playing partner. The other players who you invite besides your special playing partner can help with socializing during the round. Remember a round of eighteen holes of golf will take anywhere from three and a half to four and a half hours, and to carry the conversation the entire time yourself can be

My friendship with Stacey Mobley is a great example of the power of golf to provide access to business leadership. Stacey was the former General Counsel for Dupont, a *Fortune* Top 50 company, and the chair of the Board of Trustees for Howard University until 2020. We met back in 2012 when I showed up to play an early morning round of golf. Since I was alone, I could not schedule a tee time. Instead, I showed up at the golf course and checked in at the pro shop like everyone must do before starting their round. I was put with a twosome of players whom I did not know, Wardell Townsend and Charles Warrick. The round went well, and we had many opportunities for small talk while playing. At the end of the round, as often happens when rapport develops between players, Wardell and Charles asked me to join them for a future round.

I played several rounds after that first day with Wardell and Charles. On one occasion, Charles asked me to join him and Reggie Banks, a friend of his, for a round of golf. The round went well, and I joined Charles and Reggie for more rounds until one day Charles emailed saying that a friend of his was in town and asking if I could be the fourth player in the group along with Reggie and Stacey Mobley, a friend of theirs. I joined them for the round and played additional rounds of golf when Stacey was in town.

Eventually, the four of us started meeting regularly for dinner on Friday evenings when Stacey was visiting. The conversation was always lively and the food good, allowing rapport between all of us to grow quickly. Eventually, Stacey asked us to join him at his home in Florida for Super Bowl weekend. We flew down and had a great time and have been meeting regularly for golf, food, and good company on Super Bowl weekend ever since that first get-together.

I share this story because it illustrates how golf can provide access to business leadership. It started with showing up as a single individual looking to play and being put with two playing partners I didn't know. However, playing was only a small part of what eventually led to meeting Stacey and becoming good friends with him, Wardell, Charles, and Reggie. The formation of the relationships had nothing to do with how well or how badly we played. In fact, I cannot remember a single score from our multiple times playing together. Rather, the relationship formed because of the bond from our mutual enjoyment of golfing and the rapport developed during our shared golfing experiences.

—Eric

challenging. Thus, it's good to have other players you know in the group who can help you engage with your special playing partner during the round.

We need to point out that you don't have to make a tee time by reserving a day and time to play a round of golf. On many courses, you can be a walk-on by showing up to the clubhouse on the day you want to play and seeing if there are open time slots for your group to take for the opening hole. The attendant in the pro shop will check their time sheet to see if there's an opening for a single, two-some, or whatever number of players you have in your group. We would only advise you to walk up without a reservation if you're a single player. The attendant in the pro shop must find an opening for the number of players that you have in your group. For example, if you show up at 10:00 a.m. with two other players, there may not be a group for three players to be added to until 4:00 p.m. However, if you're a single player, you have more chances to be added to a group because you can join a group of one, two, or three. To be a walk-on, you need to go into the pro shop and let the attendant know you're a single player looking to get out and play. They may have something available immediately, or they may ask you add your name to their waiting list. It's a bit like walking into a restaurant without a reservation. You will be seated if there is a table that is unoccupied and can accommodate the size of your group. Alternatively, you may have to wait until a table with enough seats becomes available. Rather than tables, golf uses time slots and the number of players (or chairs in the restaurant comparison) to decide when you can walk on to play a round. While you're waiting, you can go out to the putting green or to the driving range, and they'll let you know when your opening comes up. We've met some great people by being added to their group. Therefore, don't hesitate to be put with a group if you're playing as a single. It's a great way to meet people that you probably wouldn't have met otherwise.

Now, let's say you call to reserve a time for four players on an upcoming Saturday morning at 8:00 a.m. Generally, the golf course will have groups go out every ten minutes, so you'll have five or six tee times that may be available in an hour. The attendant you speak with in the pro shop will give you the desired tee time if they have a spot open for four players at the requested time and day. If it's not available, they will suggest the next closest time for the number of players in your group as a possible tee time. You then decide whether to take it or not. Alternatively, if you have two players, they may say that you can join two other players at your chosen tee time or that you can go out alone as a twosome later on in the day.

Another part of the clubhouse is the food and beverage area. This is generally a good place to visit at the beginning of the round. Let's say it's an early morning round and you didn't have a chance to have breakfast. In this area, you can buy a breakfast sandwich along with coffee or some fruit juice. Most courses are designed so that you return to the clubhouse after you play the first nine holes (holes one through nine are referred to as the "front nine"). After playing the front nine, you'll arrive back at the clubhouse and can then grab something to eat or drink. One thing to remember in this situation is that you need to ensure that you buy food and beverages quickly. Otherwise, the group behind you may catch up to you while you're in the clubhouse and has the right to tee off on the tenth hole if you're still busy in the clubhouse buying something. Limit your time in the clubhouse at the turn (i.e., the changeover from playing the front nine to the back nine holes on a course) to just five to ten minutes to go in and grab something to eat or drink. Don't take too long, or you could lose your place in the playing order of groups. Once you go out and play the back nine, you'll circle back and end up back at the clubhouse. At the end of the round, the clubhouse is often referred to as the "nineteenth hole."

The third area that you'll find in most clubhouses is the locker rooms, which is where you can go to change into your golf attire before starting the round or to wash up after a round. Most golf courses have requirements when it comes to the type of clothing that you must wear when playing golf. These requirements are starting to loosen up as more young golfers start playing the game, but most courses will ask, if not require, that you wear a collared shirt, long pants (no denim), and shorts, a skirt, or a golf dress extended to the knee. If you don't have the proper attire, you can buy what you need in the pro shop if they sell it, or else you may not be allowed to play on that day unless you change your outfit. For example, the NBA legend Michael Jordan was once not allowed to play a golf course in Miami, Florida, because he wore cargo shorts.[2] Alternatively, you might run into a course that only has bathroom facilities for its locker rooms. We recommend using the locker room even if just for changing your shoes. It's generally considered bad etiquette if there is locker room with a changing area at the golf course but you decide to change your shoes and clothes in the parking lot.

Overall, there's a lot happening at the clubhouse between the pro shop, the food and beverage area, and the locker rooms. It's now time to discuss how you can be a leader at the clubhouse.

Strategy

Being strategic means that you've got a goal and a course of action to accomplish that goal. In this book, the goal is to access leadership opportunities. The way that you're going to accomplish that goal is by using golf to network with leaders who can help you advance your career toward leadership positions. Making your way to the clubhouse to start your round, you need to be clear in your own mind about your goal because it will help you in several ways from a networking perspective. For example, research suggests that having a networking goal will motivate you to build your professional network and be less concerned about what others may think of you for trying to network with them.[3] People often don't build their professional network because they're concerned that they'll be seen as opportunistic and trying to take advantage of someone for their own gain. Think about it this way: today, maybe it's the person you're thinking of playing golf with who can help you, but it could be you who can help that person in the future. Having a goal can help make this scenario a reality by motivating you to build your network today so you can help yourself and others in the future.

Having a goal is also important because it helps you assess whether to look internally to your current employer for leaders to network with using golf or whether to look externally outside your employer for leaders to invite for a round. Your professional networking opportunities will involve people located within your organization and outside your organization; knowing your goal will help you choose which to focus on in making an invitation.[4] For example, maybe you want to become informed about what's going on in other departments of your organization where leadership opportunities exist. Building relationships with people from other areas and functions of the company through shared golfing experiences can be an effective way to broaden your knowledge of the larger context in which you work and the leadership opportunities in your firm. On the other hand, maybe you're looking to get a certain leadership-related promotion within your organization. You should think about leaders in the company you could invite to play golf who can help you get the promotion, and you should be prepared to talk about why you are a good fit for the promotion during the golfing experience. Alternatively, maybe it's not a promotion, but it's just a special assignment that you seek because it will give you valuable experience that will propel you into leadership later in your career. Let's say, for example, that your employer is an international company, and you want an opportunity to work in one of their foreign branches because foreign experience is something your company looks for in its leaders. If so, find out which leaders are associated with that branch, invite them out to play golf, and see if you could use that round to learn about what is required for acquiring the assignment. During the golfing experience, share why you think you might be a good fit. All of these are internal goals, meaning goals related to what you want to achieve with a current employer.

You also may have professional goals that will require you to look externally to access a leader. Maybe you're interested in a leadership position at another firm and know that expanding your network professionally in your industry will allow you to know when leadership opportunities in the industry arise and who to contact about them. Playing a round of golf with a leader in an organization where you might want to work can be a great way to use golf to advance your career to a leadership position. Alternatively, maybe you're working in sales or marketing, where successfully acquiring leadership positions requires being successful at customer acquisition. You may want to invite a leader from an organization that you're trying to acquire as a customer and use the golfing experience as a way to develop a relationship with the leader as a first step toward persuading them to become your customer.

Curiosity

Once you have a professional goal, it's time for you to act with curiosity and identify individual leaders whom you might play golf and connect with to help you achieve your leadership goals. You'll need to identify people who play golf, because using golf to network is not going to work unless someone has an interest in the game. How do you know whether someone you're thinking of inviting plays golf? You can use your curiosity in two possible ways. The first way is through direct engagement with the person you're considering asking to play a round of golf. Through your engagement with them, you can ask questions that help you learn their interest in golf. You might, for example, ask them, "What did you do last weekend?" and listen to how they respond. Your job is to listen for whether they mention anything related to golf like playing or watching it on television. Or maybe you could ask them a more specific question, such as, "Did you watch the golf tournament over the weekend?" How they answer can reveal whether they like to watch golf. You can also look for signs in their office. Do they have any golf-related pictures or items in the office like a golf putter sitting in the corner for when they want to practice in their office? These cues will help you discover if a leader you're interested in inviting to a round of golf is interested and likely to join you on the golf course.

The second way to use your curiosity is by searching for information about the person online. Some people may call this stalking because it involves searching online to find out if there is anything connecting them with golf. However, the clues you are using are public information. For example, LinkedIn hosts many golfing groups. You can scan the LinkedIn profile for a potential special playing partner to see if they follow one of these golfing groups. Or you can look at their posts on LinkedIn or their activity on other social media platforms to see if they're posting anything related to golf. All of these could be ways that you could find out if a person you're thinking of inviting has an interest in golf. If so, then you know that's a person who's going to be a potential individual for you to invite to play golf.

Now that you've identified a leader who has an interest in golf, you need to continue to practice curiosity by asking them to join you for a round of golf. How do you make an invite? When you're going to make the invite, it should come naturally during a conversation you're having with the person. Look for those opportunities where you have an informal interaction to make the invite. If it's someone internal to your employer, maybe you pass the person in the hall or maybe you're in the elevator and you can start to have a conversation. If it's someone external, bring it up during an email exchange or phone call that lends itself to asking them to join you for a round of golf.

Regardless of the situation, you want to make sure you're direct when you make the invite. Often, people are tempted to take a less direct or an indirect approach to making requests of others.[5] The problem with indirect requests is that what you're asking is not clear. For example, you could make the invite by saying, "We should play golf sometime." Does "should" mean that you recommend they play a round of golf with you or that you're ordering them to join you for a round of golf? The word "sometime" is also problematic. Does it mean tomorrow, next week, next year, or some other time in the future? Research shows that indirect requests are less often viewed positively than more direct approaches to making requests of others.[6]

Instead of an indirect request, make a more direct request when asking a leader to play golf with you. This requires you to be explicit about what you're asking the person. Rather than saying "should," be explicit about your request by saying, "Can you join me for a round of golf?" Also, rather than saying "sometime," say "next week" so that it is clear when you would like to play golf with the person. You're more likely to get a clear yes or no from the person if you're direct, and this provides you with the information you need to either set a time for the golf outing or seek another way to develop a relationship with them. Without this type of information, if you ask in a less direct manner, you're left wondering whether the person really plans to play golf with you or just said sure because it allowed them to not commit without hurting your feelings.

You should also be intentional in communicating that you have a motive in addition to playing golf together. By intentional, we mean that you should let the person know that your intention is to use this round for professional reasons. Something like the following might work if you're seeking a new assignment: "After the round, I'd like to take a few minutes and speak with you about applying for the new assignment in our marketing department." By doing so, you let the person know that it's a round of golf, but it's also business related. This avoids any surprises when you finish the round and start to ask about the assignment. Being intentional lets you be transparent about the invite, and this helps develop trust and transparency between you and your playing partner.[7]

Adaptability

Adaptability focuses on being able to adjust your plans and respond to a situation. It is an important leadership trait in golf because your goal is to network with a leader who can help advance your career, and you will need a positive golfing experience to help you reach that goal. However, not all golf courses are the same, and not all golfers have the same skill level. This means that a golfing experience cannot be standardized but must be designed for each special playing partner you invite to play a round with you. This requires adapting to the golfing interests and ability of your special playing partner if you are to create a positive experience that will enable you to reach your goal for the round. To do so, you will need to understand your special playing partner's perspective and know the golf skill of the person you're playing with and their preferences when it comes to playing time as well as the types of courses that they're going to want to play. You need to understand these details about the person you have invited once they accept the invitation, because knowing them will lead to a better golfing experience and more cooperation on their part during the round and after.[8]

One of the easiest ways to assess someone's skill level is to ask them their handicap. It's not a negative question when you ask somebody about their golf handicap. You're not suggesting there's some special challenge the person experiences. In the game of golf, the handicapping system assigns a value indicating how much above par a golfer scores on average. A handicap officially gets assessed by playing tournaments or by the clubhouse assessing your performance and calculating your average from the rounds you have played. Each hole on a golf course has a par score indicating how many strokes a golfer is expected to take to advance the ball from the tee box starting the hole to the hole on the green. A regulation course has eighteen holes that vary in the number of holes that are par 3, par 4, and par 5. "Par for the course" is the sum of pars for each of the eighteen holes on the course. In the context of a golf handicap, if the course has a par of 72 and you typically shoot an 82, then your handicap is going to be 10. Thus, if you ask your special playing partner, "What's your handicap?" and they say, "My handicap is 20," this means that the person typically shoots a 92 on a par 72 course. The average amateur male golfer shoots a score of 90 while the average female golfer shoots 108.[9] A good strategy is to choose an easier course if your invited person has a higher handicap.

Not all golfers have a formal handicap because obtaining one requires registering, either at a golf club or online. If you register for a handicap at a golf course, once you play a round, you then enter your score along with information about the course into a computer system maintained by the course. Your golf rounds do not have to be played at the same course where you're registered for a handicap, but you will need to register all of your rounds through the course's system. Those scores are then shared with the state golf association for the golf course where you're registered, and your handicap is calculated by the association and reported to your club for distribution to you. You will be required to play a minimum number of rounds, usually five, before a handicap can be calculated for you. Alternatively, you can register with an online service rather than a golf club. Once you post the required number of golf scores, the online service will issue you a handicap.

Sometimes the person you invite may not have subscribed to a handicap service and will not have a formal handicap number to share with you. In that case, ask them what they usually shoot and do your own math to figure out their playing ability. For example, if they usually shoot in the 80s, then you know they are a good golfer because they score lower than the average for most golfers and would likely appreciate a more challenging golf course to play.

Knowing your special playing partner's handicap, you can start to choose a course that fits with their golfing ability. This requires identifying the slope of the courses you're considering using for the golfing experience. All golf courses have a slope, which indicates the difficulty of the course. The slope is determined by the USGA, which is the governing body for golf in the United States and Mexico. There are multiple sets of tees you can play on a golf course (we'll have more to say about this when we discuss leadership at the tee box), and each set of tees have a slope value that tells you which sets are more or less difficult to play during your round. If the slope for a set of tees is 135, then you know playing that set of tees is going to be challenging because the average slope for all golf courses is 120.[10] If you're planning to play with someone who isn't that skilled of a golfer, don't choose a course with a high slope because they will likely struggle to play the round, which will only result in them feeling embarrassed, frustrated, or angry. These types of experiences are not good for successful networking. Rather, you want a course that you both are going to enjoy playing because a positive golfing experience is more likely to result in a positive networking opportunity. Thus, you want to make sure that you're choosing courses that are good matches for the skill level of the person whom you're playing with.

In addition to adapting your course selection to your special playing partner's skill level, you should also adapt it to their course style and time preferences. Is there a style of course they want to play? The two most common styles of golf courses are parkland and links courses. A parkland-style golf course is inland and away from the seacoast. It will have many trees and bushes that make the course very scenic but also present hazards on the golf course. Alternatively, a links course is typically close to the seacoast and has few trees and bushes. It offers scenic coastal vistas and rolling fairways. Rather than having trees and bushes for hazards, a links course relies on elements like wind and sand to create hazards on the golf course. As for tee times, you'll need to ask your playing partner whether weekdays or weekends are better and whether mornings or afternoon are better. Typically, weekend mornings are the more popular days and times, so you'll need to plan well in advance if these represent your special playing partner's preferences.

How do you determine your playing partner's course and time preferences? If you're in their office when you make the invite, you can look for pictures of golf courses on their desk or wall. If you see trees, you know they like parkland courses, whereas if the pictures contain rolling sand dunes next to the ocean, then they would probably like to play a links course. You can also ask them about the last course they played or the best round they ever played. Once you have this information, you can search the course online to get a sense of their style preference. You could also ask them if they're a member of a club and ask if it's a parkland course. If they are a member of a parkland-style course, then you should suggest a parkland-style course for your round with them. For learning their time preferences, ask which days or times work best for them. Once you have the required information, you're ready to design the golfing experience so that it fits with your special playing partner's skill level and golfing preferences, setting the stage for a successful golfing and networking experience.

Empowerment

You also want to act in a manner that empowers your special playing partner as they prepare to meet you at the clubhouse and start the golfing experience. Creating an environment for success is empowering for both you and your special playing partner. Doing so will give them a sense of confidence and choice in the golfing experience that will motivate greater cooperation and commitment.[11] You can be empowering in two ways. The first involves logistics. With respect to the clubhouse, that means providing your special playing partner with the information they need to be prepared when they arrive at the golf course. First, you always want to share your phone number with them so that, if they are running late or maybe get lost on the way, they have a way to easily contact you. You should also give them directions or, at a minimum, give them the address so that they can use GPS to easily find the golf course. Second, you should advise them if there is a dress code for the golf course. This is something you should ask about when you call the pro shop to make your tee time. You should also let your playing partner know if there is a locker room where they can change clothing before or after the round. Third, you should tell them if there's going to be a practice green and driving range on the course. These are all important items that help them be prepared for what they will experience when they arrive.

It is also important to recommend a place where you will meet them. A good meeting place is the bag drop area in the parking lot. Most courses will have a structure where you can unload your golf bag when you arrive. Often, there will be an attendant who can help with unloading golf bags at this area. This is a good place to meet because it is centrally located near the arrival area in the parking lot. It also gives you a chance to greet your special playing partner upon their arrival and ensure the golfing experience gets off to a good start. You'll want to avoid having them wandering around looking for you, so setting a meeting place like the bag drop is highly recommended. Other good meeting places include the pro shop and putting green. Be sure your special playing partner is empowered with the knowledge needed to easily find these places.

The other empowering information to share with your playing partner is what type of event you have invited them to. You could invite them to a charity event where proceeds from the event like green fees or food and beverage purchases are donated to one or more nonprofits featured at the event. Charity golfing events are very common because charitable activity is a big part of the golfing industry. Professional golf tournaments annually donate more to charities than Major League Baseball, the National Football League, and the National Basketball League combined.[12] The charity aspect of golf is not limited to professional golf but also occurs in amateur golf when nonprofits hold golfing tournaments as fundraisers. This means there are a lot of charity golf tournaments, and you might invite someone you want to network with to one. Asking someone to join you at a charity event is a nice invite because not only are you and your special playing partner enjoying a round of golf together, but you're also playing golf for a good cause that will benefit others. However, charity events often ask for a donation, and you need to make sure your special playing partner knows ahead of time if there is such an expectation. The last thing you want is for them to arrive and find out they need to hand over a donation when they aren't prepared to do so.

Alternatively, your invite can be for a special playing partner to join you for a friendly round with you and a couple of other players who will be in the foursome. Make sure you let them know the names of the other players. Remember, always try to have a foursome so that all the pressure to carry the conversation is not on you during the round.

You can also be empowering in the course you select for the golfing experience. There is a history of social exclusion with golf in its relationship with women and people of color,[13] and that exclusion is one reason why only 23 percent of all golfers are female and only 18 percent of golfers are people of color.[14] Some golf courses are going to be more welcoming of women and people of color than others. If you or your special playing partner is a woman or a person of color, you can empower yourself and the special playing partner by selecting a course that is friendly to women and people of color. What are some indicators of a friendly course? Look at the website and the staff listed for the course. The presence of women and people of color on the staff is a strong signal that the course will be more open to female players and golfers of color. Another good indicator is the makeup of the club membership. Also, examine the events calendar if there is one on the website. Do you see any events for women? If so, then it is probably a friendly course for female golfers in your group. You can also see what merchandise from the pro shop is advertised on the website. Merchandise that is only for men is reason to question the friendliness of the course and whether playing there will be empowering to you or your special playing partner if either of you are a woman.

Integrity

You've established your goal for the outing and shown leadership in choosing a playing partner who can help you reach that goal. You made the invite in a direct and intentional way, and it was accepted. You then chose a course and tee time based on your playing partner's skill and preferences. You empowered your special playing partner with the information they needed to arrive prepared for the round of golf. The next leadership trait you need to demonstrate is integrity. Doing so requires you to follow the rules and etiquette of golf related to the clubhouse and follow through on what you committed to with your special playing partner. The first act of integrity at the clubhouse is to arrive early and before your special playing partner arrives for the round. It's recommended that you arrive at least forty-five minutes before your tee time. Doing so helps in several ways. First, it allows you to follow through on your commitment to meet your playing partner at the predetermined meeting place. You don't want your playing partner waiting for you to arrive. This can only lead to confusion on the part of your playing partner and does not show your integrity. To make sure you arrive first, when you share information about the tee time with your playing partner, ask what time they plan to arrive. This gives you the information you need to make sure you act with integrity by arriving first. Showing this type of integrity is important because it will positively impact your special playing partner's perception of you as a leader who can be trusted to carry through with what they said they would do, and this will be the kind of person they will want to network with and help over time.[15]

Second, arriving early gives you plenty of time to check in with the pro shop and let them know you're present and when you expect the other people in the group to arrive. This is also when you would pay for your round and the round of your playing partner and others in the group, if you plan to do so. It is generally advisable to pay for your invited special playing partner and possibly the other players in the group, especially if they've made special arrangements to join you for the round. While you're checking in at the clubhouse, be sure to ask if there are any special rules on the course for the day. For example, if it's been a very rainy day, the golf course may require you to keep golf carts on the cart path rather than drive them down the fairway like you can during better weather. The course may also have special rules on the day of the outing that allow you to lift, clean, and replace the ball because the rain has made the course muddy, making it likely your ball may be embedded within the ground or end up in a puddle of water on the fairway. You can find out if there are special rules for the day by asking in the pro shop, and then you should advise your special playing partner and others in the group of these special rules.

Mindfulness

The final leadership trait that is important at the clubhouse is mindfulness, which requires you to stay in the moment at the clubhouse and focus on why you've created the golfing experience. To do so, you'll first need to remember that you're at the golf course to reach your professional goal that you set out to achieve when you decided to make the golfing invite. This means that personal goals related to your golfing performance should not be primary in your mind. Instead, creating a positive golfing experience for your invited playing partner and using the experience to build your network and advance your career toward leadership opportunities should remain top of mind. You're the host, and you should act like it by supporting your invited special playing partner rather than focusing on your own experience and golf performance.

Make sure you meet them at the designated spot at the designated time. When you do, be mindful that the golfing experience has formally begun and you need to start engaging with your special playing partner. This will involve small talk that is spontaneous and situational to what is happening in the moment.[16] For example, if your plan involves meeting them at the bag drop, you might compliment them on their clubs and ask them how long they've had them. You could also ask what they like about the clubs and where they purchased them. Spend time preparing a greeting, general observations, and questions that you can ask when your special playing partner arrives to start the engagement. Once started, you will then engage in small talk based on what is happening around you and your prepared questions.

However, you must be mindful of which conversational topics are appropriate at the clubhouse when you start your round and which topics should stay out of the conversation until after the round. To help you consider this, think of the possible topics for your conversations falling along a continuum with social topics at one end and business topics at the other end.[17] Social topics are of a more personal nature, like getting to know what your special playing partner likes to do for fun, how they are feeling that day, and where they went to college. Business topics might include asking about a new opportunity in the company if your goal is a promotion or assignment with your current employer. Another possible topic may be the business performance of your special playing partner's company if the goal is to acquire their business as a new customer. Or maybe you've read something about their business that you can ask them about. These are all examples of business topics you may discuss during the golfing experience.

You should be mindful and spend more time on social topics and less time on business topics at the clubhouse. Focusing on social topics will allow you to start the process of building rapport with your special playing partner much faster than starting with business topics. One reason why is that starting with business topics sends a strong signal that you're only there for yourself. Your special playing partner knows there is a professional motivation behind the golfing experience. You were intentional and made that clear when you made the invite. However, you also asked them to share in the social experience that comes with spending time playing a round of golf together. Be mindful of that in your conversation at the clubhouse.

Another reason for waiting to discuss business topics later during the golfing experience is that the answer might be negative, and this can ruin the rest of the experience. For example, maybe you're interested in acquiring a playing partner as a new client. You ask, "Are you considering new suppliers?" and they may say "Nope. We've decided to only work with our existing suppliers in the coming year." That negative response means that your goal of acquiring the special playing partner's business as a new customer is highly unlikely. Does that mean the golf outing should end? If that was the only reason you invited them, then there is a reason to think it should. However, you would miss the opportunity to network and learn more about the person and possibly other ways they could help you and you might be able to help them professionally. Yet by asking a business question and getting a negative response, you've created an awkward situation that is going to make it harder to reap the networking benefits golf offers.

These reasons for holding off talking about business until after the round are important to remember. But they do not mean that business should never be discussed at the clubhouse or during the round. You should talk business if your special playing partner brings it up. For example, they might add to their greeting at the meeting area near the bag drop that they're looking forward to learning more about your company and how it might help their company as a supplier. When your special playing partner opens the door to discussing business, you should take advantage of the opportunity. The mindful way is to wait and let the playing partner bring up business and then follow through.

As we've seen, a lot is happening at the clubhouse, and there can be many challenges in making this time effective for networking with leaders and accessing leadership opportunities. We've discussed how you can be a leader at this spot in the golf experience by drawing on your leadership traits related to strategy, curiosity, adaptability, empowerment, integrity, and mindfulness. Next up is the practice area. Let's head over there and discuss how you can be a leader in that leadership moment during the golfing experience.

Leadership at the Practice Area

Most golf courses feature a practice area where you can warm up before starting your round of golf. Generally, the practice area will be located somewhere near the clubhouse or the first hole. The practice area will have one or a combination of three different areas. There will almost always be a driving range where you can hit your wedges, irons, and woods using a full swing. This is where you can practice just about any shot except putting. In this area, there will be a bag stand where you can put your golf bag while you hit balls on the driving range, which can be grass or an artificial mat. A grass driving range means that you're going to be hitting off the ground. You also can tee up the ball to hit your driver. Don't worry about making a divot in the ground. The course regularly reseeds these areas so the grass will grow back. If it's an artificial mat, you'll be standing on and hitting off what is essentially a hard carpet. There will be a rubber tee for teeing the ball on the mat and a rectangular tray next to the mat where you can place your range balls while you're practicing.

Many practice areas will also have a section specifically designated for practicing your putting. In this area, you will find a practice putting green with multiple holes that allow many people to simultaneously practice their putting stroke. At many courses, you can also practice chipping and pitching on the putting green. However, this is not the case at all courses. The course will indicate on signage around the putting green if you are not allowed to hit practice pitch shots and chip shots. Another way you can tell if pitching and chipping are allowed on the putting green is to look for a sand trap next to the putting green because hitting from the sand is a form of pitching and having a sand trap next to the putting green means the course allows you to hit pitch shots onto it. To ensure you're following course rules, be sure to check for signage around the putting green. If you don't see any, then it's acceptable to practice your pitching and chipping on the putting green.

Some courses will also have a third section of the practice area solely for the purpose of practicing your pitch and chip shots. This will often be the case when the course does not allow these shots to be practiced around the putting green. If there is a specific area for practicing pitch and chip shots, it will most often be a green with a single hole in it and a flag in the hole.

You will typically use your own balls on the putting green and for chipping around the putting green, but it is not common practice to take your own balls to the practice area and hit them on the range. Instead, some courses will include range balls with the green fee you pay to play the course. Be sure to ask when you make your tee time or pay your green fee if balls for the practice area are included in the green fee. If this is the case, range balls will already be on the driving range for you to hit. Hit as many as you want but be sure not to take any with you when leaving the range. It is not good golf etiquette to take balls provided by the course from the practice area, so just enjoy hitting them for practice.

Most golf courses will not provide golf balls in the practice area, and you will need to buy them. The place to buy range balls for the practice area is the pro shop in the clubhouse. To order range balls, most people say something like, "Can I get a bucket of balls for the range?" or "Can I get some range balls?" to the attendant working in the pro shop. You'll then be asked what size you want. Range balls can be bought in small (usually around forty to sixty balls), medium (usually around sixty to eighty balls), or large buckets (usually eighty balls or more). The cost varies with size. Medium or large buckets are good when you have a longer time for practicing. Once you purchase range balls, you'll either be given a bucket of balls in the pro shop or you may be given a token that you can use at a kiosk located near the practice area to retrieve your range balls. At the kiosk, there will be buckets or baskets of different sizes. You'll need to put the bucket for the size you purchased under the opening of the ball dispenser. Balls will fall from the opening in the kiosk once you insert the token, so be sure to place your bucket where the balls come out before you put in your token. Otherwise, your balls will go everywhere as they get dispensed. Trust me, we speak from experience when we say this can happen. It can be a little awkward, but if it happens to you, just pick up your balls and head to the driving range.

We've covered many of the logistical issues associated with the practice area. It's now time to talk about practicing leadership in this area to ensure the round is most effective from a leadership and networking perspective.

Strategy

Being in the practice area means that you're just about to start the round with your special playing partner, and you may be nervous, especially if you're playing with someone like the president of your company or the CEO of a firm you hope to acquire as a customer. Maybe it's one of your first times playing a full round of golf. No matter the situation, it's natural that you would start to get a little nervous in anticipation of the round.

One of your goals in the practice area will be to prepare yourself to play in an acceptable manner. It is best practice to establish a playing goal to focus and mitigate nervousness about a round. Spending time in the practice area on shots that will help you achieve that goal can bring focus to your game. Remember, your intent is not to shoot your best round, but you do want to play in an acceptable manner that's going to allow you to play the round at an acceptable pace.

One way to approach achieving this goal is to allot your time in the practice area based on the likelihood that you will need to hit each type of shot. That means you should spend the most time in the practice area on putting. Take the example of Tiger Woods, undoubtedly one of the greatest golfers of all time. He has a standard routine for warming up before he plays a round. He always starts and ends with putting and dedicates the most time to it. In between, he will hit his irons and woods, but the major focus of his warm-up is putting.[1]

In addition to a playing goal, you should also aim to nurture a relationship with your special playing partner in the practice area in a purposeful and informal way. Your goal is purposeful in the sense that you are seeking to have your special playing partner start to share information about their daily life, such as how often they play golf, how long they've worked in their current job, and where they went to college. Getting them to share information about themselves enables you to identify common interests that you can discuss during the round when you're standing on the tee box, riding in the golf cart between shots, or walking up to the green.

Getting your special playing partner to share information about themselves requires that you engage with them in an informal way that signals your genuine interest in them and the golfing experience.[2] There are many ways to be informal. One way is through the use of humor in sharing your own mistakes. For example, suppose you are in the stall beside your special playing partner on the driving range and you hit a wayward shot. You can casually share your hope that you're getting those shots out of your system before the round begins. Another option is to ask your special playing partner how they're hitting the ball. These types of informal comments and questions are important for starting the process of building a relationship with your special playing partner.

Mindfulness

Leadership in the practice area also requires acting in a way that brings you fully into the moment at hand. Warming up by hitting balls or putting is an important way to get yourself physically ready. However, you also want to get your mind ready. Suzy Whaley has emphasized the importance of getting your mind ready to play. Suzy is a PGA Master Professional. The PGA is the largest sports organization in the world, with over twenty-nine thousand members who are certified as experts in teaching the game of golf. Being a PGA Master Professional means that Suzy is one of only a handful of PGA members who have achieved the highest level of teaching expertise. Suzy is not only an expert golf instructor. She also has the distinction of being the first and only woman president of the PGA since she was elected to the position in November of 2018. One practice that Suzy emphasizes with her students is to visually imagine the shots you will play in the round.[3] The emphasis should be on visualizing what you want to happen rather than what you fear will happen. For instance, don't just hit one drive after the other in the practice area. Think about the first hole and visualize what type of drive you want to hit on that hole. Doing so will prepare you both physically and mentally for the round.

Visualization is a powerful technique used by public speakers, musicians, actors, and dancers to bring calm and focus to the delivery of their performance. You can use visualization both in your preparation before the round in the practice area and as you prepare to engage with your special playing partner. What do you want to know about them? What do you want them to know about you? What is the quality of the experience you hope the two of you will have during the round? Setting clear intentions for all aspects of the round can greatly enhance your experience.

You also want to be mindful that a round of golf is about to begin and gather several pieces of equipment that you will need during the round. One is to ensure that you have a ball marker for the green. You don't want to realize on the green that you don't have a way to mark your ball, especially if your ball happens to be in the putting line of your special playing partner. You'll have to delay play by going back to the cart and getting a marker if you aren't mindful in the practice area and put one in your pocket where you can easily get to it when you're on the green. If you do have to go back to the cart to get a ball marker, it sends a strong signal to your special playing partner that you're not prepared for the round, and you don't want that to be one of their first impressions of you. For similar reasons, you should also be mindful to check that you have tees for teeing up the ball on the tee boxes.

You also need to make sure you have sufficient golf balls for the outing. It can be very embarrassing to run out of golf balls during the round because it means that you must borrow some from your special playing partner. Having to borrow from your playing partner also puts them in danger of running out of golf balls, which could force them to stop playing. Avoid this situation by carrying several golf balls in your bag. How many is sufficient depends on your playing ability. Better players need to carry fewer golf balls, whereas beginners should carry more.

Lastly, you should put your phone on mute for the round. Everyone knows how distracting a ringing phone can be at work or at home. Double or triple that on the golf course, where playing requires your full concentration. Not turning off your phone ringer also signals to your playing partner that you're not 100 percent focused on the golfing experience, which can cause your special playing partner to question the genuineness of your interest in spending time with them. In fact, you should even consider putting your phone in your bag, based on research showing that the mere presence of a mobile phone can make it difficult for close relationships to develop.[4]

In addition to helping prepare you for the upcoming round, being mindful and making sure you have a ball marker, tees, and golf balls can create opportunities for you to further nurture the relationship with your special playing partner. This opportunity is based on the idea of reciprocity, meaning that we like to treat others as they have treated us. Research suggests that humans are internally motivated to act in ways that follow reciprocity whether they are treated well (doing good for others in return for the good they have done to us) or badly (doing badly unto others in return for the bad they have done to us).[5] While you may want to avoid needing to borrow tees or golf balls from your special playing partner, having this equipment ready and available allows you to help your playing partner if they leave the practice area without them. Helping your special playing partner when they need a tee, ball marker, or golf ball can have several relational benefits. First, it provides you with an opportunity to do your special playing partner a favor. The human desire to act in a reciprocal manner means that your special playing partner will likely seek opportunities to repay the favor on the course or potentially later off the course. True, giving someone a golf tee is a small favor, but that doesn't mean that the repaying of that favor will also be small. People mentally calculate the value of favors given to them and seek to repay them at an equal or higher value to avoid being seen as ungrateful or even unfair.[6] As a result, giving a tee to your special playing partner when they need one can be like the acorn that turns into an oak tree, setting into motion the opportunity for your special playing partner to repay the favor in a way that can benefit your career in the future.

Second, doing your special playing partner a favor helps build trust in the relationship. Giving your special playing partner something without asking for anything in return reflects your willingness to help the person. Being helpful signals that you value their best interest and are not simply using them for your own gain. This promotes an emotional bond between people that contributes to a belief that people will act to support each other in the future, which is a critical component of trust-building in relationships.[7] Thus, your small act of helping your special playing partner can begin the process of strengthening the relationship by increasing your special playing partner's trust in you.

Third, by helping your special playing partner, you are modeling helping behavior in the relationship, and this gives a sense of direction to the relationship as it develops on and off the course. On the course, you will interact with your special playing partner many times, and there will likely be several opportunities for your special playing partner to repay the favor by helping you find a wayward shot. These small acts of helping each other will result in a relationship characterized by reciprocity during the round and into the future.[8]

Curiosity

Curiosity in the practice area is about using your time to learn about your special playing partner's golf game. The best way to do this is to give some attention to how your special playing partner hits the ball on the driving range. Don't stop what you're doing in the practice area to watch your special playing partner, but you do want to gain a sense of their ball flight by casually and informally seeing how they're hitting balls on the driving range. Obtaining this information is important because it will provide insight into the character of your special playing partner. For example, if your special playing partner told you they usually shoot a score of 80, then you should expect the person to hit the ball well, given that par for a course is usually 72 strokes. However, if you notice your special playing partner hitting the ball poorly on the range, then it may be a clue that your special playing partner will play poorly that day. If so, this could lead them to be in a negative mood during the round. Knowing this information can help you prepare for dealing with this type of situation.

The other reason you'll want to be curious about your special playing partner's practice is because it will enable you to be a better playing partner on the course. No one hits every shot perfectly, and very few people hit every shot straight. We all hit bad shots, and we all tend to hit the golf ball with a certain shape or curvature. By knowing your special playing partner's typical ball flight, you'll be better able to help them track the flight of their ball when they hit it, enabling you to help them find their ball more effectively when it goes astray. To do this, we need to understand a bit about the different types of ball flight.

A golfer typically hits the ball on a right-to-left or left-to-right flight path. Let's start with ball flights that move from left to right because there are several different types of this ball flight and they each have a special name in golf. To help with describing the different ball flights, imagine you are a right-handed golfer hitting a drive from the tee box and aiming for the center of the fairway. A drive that goes immediately right of the center of the fairway and does not curve very much is called a push shot. (If you're a left-handed golfer, think of the golf ball going left of the center of the fairway.) Alternatively, the ball may start straight down the fairway when you hit it with the driver but then begin to curve right and keep curving right. That is called a slice shot. The other type of left-to-right ball flight is the fade shot. This ball flight occurs when the ball starts slightly left of the center of the fairway when you strike it but then curves right until it ends up in the center of the fairway.

Using the same imaginary experience of hitting a drive from the tee box, it is also possible to describe typical ball flights that move from right to left. A drive that goes immediately left of the center of the fairway and stays straight as it flies in the air is called a pull shot. The ball may start straight down the fairway when hit from the tee box but then start turning left. If so, then the ball flight is referred to as a hook shot. The ball may also follow what is referred to as a draw ball flight, where the ball starts slightly right of the center of the fairway when driven from the tee box but then curves left until it ends up in the center of the fairway.

Knowing the typical ball flight of your special playing partner will allow you to know how much help your special playing partner may need in tracking and finding their ball during the round. For example, push or pull shots often miss the fairway and are more likely to end up in the woods or in a hazard. Alternatively, fade and draw shots typically end up on target and a player who hits these types of shots will need less help. Helping your special playing partner who hits a draw or slice shot will depend upon how much the ball curves and whether they account for the flight path in their aim. The more the ball curves left or right, the more you will probably need to help your special playing partner during the round.

Knowing the names of the different ball flights will also help you understand what is being said and discussed about golf both on and off the course. Most people use the names for the different ball flights rather than describe them. For example, you are more likely to hear someone say, "I pushed it" when asked where the ball went rather than, "It went right and stayed pretty straight." Off the course, you are also more likely to hear people describe the path of a golf shot using the name rather than providing a description of the ball flight. People at work, for instance, are more likely to say, "He hooked it into the water" rather than, "The ball went straight and then turned to the left before going into the water."

You should also use your curiosity to learn about your special playing partner's pace of play. If they get on the range and proceed to go through a bucket of balls at a rapid pace, then it's a good bet that they are going to be a fast player. On the other hand, they probably will have a slower pace of play on the course if they take a lot of time between hitting each ball on the driving range or putting each ball on the practice green. This information can help you understand what to expect timewise for the round and what your special playing partner might expect of you regarding pace of play.

Adaptability

The practice area is also where you'll need to practice adaptability. One type of adjustment involves the way in which you interact with your special playing partner. The time you spend communicating with them on the golf course is going to provide many opportunities to develop a professional relationship between the two of you. Taking advantage of these opportunities requires that you make subtle adjustments to the language you use, and the best time to start doing that is in the practice area, where you have the first opportunity to start sharing the golfing experience.

Strong relationships are built on trust, and one of the factors that will influence the trust your special playing partner has in you is the degree to which they see similarities between themselves and you.[9] Similarity is important to the development of trust because it can result in your special playing partner expecting that the two of you share beliefs about acceptable behavior and goals in the relationship. It can also lead them to have greater confidence that you are not solely in the moment for your benefit but have their interests in mind too.

This golf story comes from the experience of Dr. Carolyn Massiah, current associate chair for the Department of Marketing and a lecturer in marketing at the University of Central Florida's College of Business.[14] Carolyn learned to play golf when she was in the Air Force as an officer's wife. On one occasion, she went golfing with a group of officers' wives. She was one of the younger people in the group and the only person of color. The course they were playing maintained a beverage station in the practice area where golfers could buy something to drink while practicing before a round. The only people in any type of uniform on the range at the time were working in the beverage area and were wearing black pants, a white shirt, and a bow tie.

On her way to the first tee, Carolyn's group stopped at the beverage counter in the practice area to buy a beverage to drink during the round. The day had been hot, and the counter was low on drinks, so the people working the counter had gone to restock. As she was standing by the beverage counter waiting for the staff to return, a white man approached the counter and turned to Carolyn to say, "Are you bringing more beverages?" Carolyn responded, "Well, I don't know when they're bringing beverages back, but I suppose they're coming sometime soon." Not satisfied with her answer, the man proceeded to ask Carolyn, "Well, can you go and get some now?" Turning her full attention to the man, Carolyn told him, "I don't work here. I'm golfing just like you." Surprised by the answer, he said, "Really?" Carolyn reiterated what she had said earlier, "I really don't work here. I'm golfing just like you." Carolyn and the man stood in silence until the beverage staff returned, allowing each to buy their beverage and head back to their respective groups.

You may also need to adapt if your special playing partner is not able to join you in the practice area. Your special playing partner may arrive late, for instance, because they got held up at the office or took a wrong turn on their way to the golf course. Their lateness can mean that there is not sufficient time before your tee time for them to go to the practice area. One adjustment to make in this situation is to spend time at the practice area before your special playing partner arrives. Remember, you should arrive early, at least thirty to forty-five minutes before your tee time. If your special playing partner is late to the designated meeting spot, call them and ask about their arrival time. If they are going to be late, head to the range and spend the time you have before they arrive warming up. However, remember to stay in contact with them and leave the range in time to meet them when they do arrive.

It's also possible that your special playing partner may not want to go to the practice area, and this can require adaptation on your part. In that case, one option is to find the starter and ask if you can go out early. A starter is a person stationed near the first hole who checks that groups are teeing off at the right time and makes sure that everyone in the group has paid for their round in the pro shop. You'll usually find the starter in a small shack or sitting in a golf cart close to the first hole. You can approach the starter if your special playing partner does not want to practice and ask if there is a tee time open before your scheduled tee time so that your group could start early. There may be an opportunity to do this if there aren't a lot of groups playing that day or if there have been cancellations.

You may not be able to tee off early. In that case, you can use the time while you wait to get food or drinks in the pro shop and spend time getting to know more about your special playing partner. To help you with this situation if it arises, prepare some questions you want to ask before you arrive for the golfing experience. Be ready with social questions like, "What brought you to the area?" and golf questions like, "How did you first learn to play the game?" These questions will enable you to start engaging with your special playing partner and developing the relationship.

Integrity

Integrity is important at every leadership moment, but the practice area is the first time you will be on the course among other golfers, and this can create situations for microaggressions to occur that require integrity to face. "Microaggression" is a term used to describe subtle forms of racism and sexism that people in under-represented groups often experience.[10] Different types of microaggressions include microassaults, microinsults, and microinvalidations.[11]

The man's behavior does not fall into the category of a microassault because it did not appear to be a conscious effort on his part to demean or insult Carolyn. He didn't use a racial epithet or assault her. It is also not a microinvalidation because the man did not attempt to invalidate Carolyn's experience as a woman and a person of color by saying something that denied her experiences such as, "There are no Black people, just people." Rather, the man appeared to be oblivious to the fact that he had made an erroneous assumption that Carolyn, as a woman and a person of color, was a member of the beverage service crew. Making this microaggression even more apparent was that Carolyn had on her golf attire and in no way was dressed like the service staff.

People from underrepresented groups don't just experience microaggressions on the golf course. Unfortunately, they are part of their everyday experience. The constant experience of microaggressions forces people from underrepresented groups to learn how to deal with them. Parents and other family members teach young people from underrepresented groups how to react to these things. The point of this discussion is not to bring awareness of the existence of microaggressions but rather to describe the types of microaggressions you may experience in the practice area and on the golf course, in general, so that you can be prepared and not let them interfere with achieving the goal you've set for the golfing experience. This discussion also aims to help white men be allies on the golf course by increasing awareness of the presence of microaggressions.

On the golf course, the three most likely types of microaggressions someone may experience focus on roles, ability, and membership. Examples of role-related microaggressions include having a Black man mistaken for a caddie rather than a golfer and a woman mistaken for a service worker rather than a golfer. Ability-related microaggressions focus on golf skills as reflected in statements like, "I'm surprised how well you play" or "Wow, you hit it a long way for a woman." Microaggressions can also question whether one belongs on the golf course. Men rolling their eyes when a woman walks up to the tee and a person of color being asked to verify their membership in a club when white people aren't required to do the same are both examples of people from underrepresented groups experiencing microaggressions related to whether they belong on the course.

There are ways you can respond to microaggressions you may experience or witness. These suggestions aren't meant to replace what you may have already learned about successfully dealing with microaggressions. Rather, they are shared with the intent of broadening the options you have for effectively responding on the golf course. Research has identified two options that are effective in these situations: making the invisible visible and disarming the microaggression.[12] Making the invisible visible recognizes that sometimes these microaggressions aren't conscious, but awareness about them needs to occur to change them. For example, if you're a woman and you're told, "I'm surprised how well you hit the ball," respond by thanking the person for the compliment but also bring awareness to their false assumption about women's playing ability by asking, "Why are you surprised?" This puts it back on the person making the statement to explain and will bring awareness to their faulty thinking. As another example of this approach, imagine someone assumes you are a server and proceeds to ask you for a drink. You can respond by turning to them and asking, "Are we taking turns? I'm getting this round, and you're picking up the tab for the next round?"

The second approach is to disarm the microaggression, and this approach focuses on making the perpetrator aware of the harm associated with their microaggression and forcing them to confront it. To illustrate, reconsider Carolyn's experience described earlier. A way to disarm the microaggression would be for Carolyn to say something along the lines of, "Ouch! Why don't you think I'm here to play golf?" to the man when he asked her to get him a drink. By doing so, the man would be made aware that his statement was hurtful because of the assumption it made about Carolyn as a woman and a person of color. Research suggests that increasing awareness can help limit an individual's microaggressions in the future.[13]

Another way to implement the technique of disarming the microaggression is to describe what is happening to the perpetrator of a microaggression. Referring to Carolyn's experience again, we can see her response falling into this category when she says, "I don't work here. I'm golfing just like you" to the man after he first asks her about the beverage service. This would have made it obvious that she was not a part of the beverage staff but a golfer wanting a beverage just like him.

Any of these approaches will be helpful. Even more important is to remember that you belong on the golf course. You have as much right to be there as anyone else, and it is not your responsibility to change people's minds. Your responsibility is to make them aware when they have acted in a way that does not show integrity toward you. Change is slow in this space. Fortunately, the LPGA and PGA have created more initiatives that are trying to change the face of golf, so the industry is putting time and energy into addressing these issues. Never forget you belong.

Empowerment

Empowerment and making sure to enable yourself and your playing partner to play in a self-directed manner is also important when you're at the practice area. One way you can empower yourself and your special playing partner is by having the information needed to play each hole and make your way around the golf course. An easy way to do this is to make sure that you have a scorecard before you leave the practice area to begin your round. The scorecard will provide you and your special playing partner with the distance and par of each hole. This information will enable you and your special playing partner to strategize well as you play the course.

Some courses also have GPS installed in each golf cart, and this can be empowering by allowing you to instantly know yardage from your ball to the hole or provision you a visual representation of the layout for a hole. The GPS is a little screen that's hung from the ceiling of the golf cart, and for each hole it will track your position on the golf course and tell you at any spot how far you are from the hole. Even if your cart has a GPS, we recommend that you still have a scorecard because you never know when the GPS may stop working. Another reason to still get a scorecard is you'll need it to enter the score for each hole.

The other way you will be able to learn yardage on the course is by using the yardage markers that are typically posted on each hole. The yardage markers can vary in how they are presented. They may be colored circles or rectangles embedded in the ground in the fairway. You might also see yardage markers that are colored stakes stuck into the ground in the fairway or along the edge of the fairways. Red yardage markers, whether a circle, rectangle, or stake, mean that you have 100 yards to the center of the green. If you see a white yardage marker, it means the center of the green is 150 yards away. A blue yardage marker in the fairway indicates 200 yards from the center of the green. Generally, you won't see yardage markers farther out than 200 yards. You should ask the starter or the attendant in the pro shop what types of yardage markers a golf course uses before starting a round so that you and your special playing partner can easily determine the distance of your shots to the green as you play the round.

Another piece of information that is empowering to know before you start a round of golf is the pin locations on the green. The pin locations tell you where on the green the pin is located: front of the green, middle of the green, or back of the green. The color of the flag will change depending on where the pin is located. Although these colors are not universal, a red flag will often mean that the pin is in the front of the green. A white flag is commonly used to mark a pin in the middle of the green, while a blue tee indicates the flag is in the back of the green. Make sure to ask in the pro shop or ask the starter about the pin location and whether flag colors used by the golf course.

Some golf courses will indicate pin location using letters or numbers rather than flag colors. If this is the case, there will be a figure on the scorecard for each green with letters or numbers showing different areas of the green. On any given day, the course will use an individual number or letter to indicate pin position. For example, if a course is playing a "1" pin location, then the pin will be located on each green where a "1" is shown on the scorecard for the green. Generally, you should ask when you start the round what pin markers are used so that you and your special playing partner will be empowered to select the right shot to hit.

You and your special playing partner will be most empowered by using the pin locations and yardage markers together when making your shot selection. You do this by starting first with the distance of the yardage marker. Then, you add, subtract, or make no change to the yardage based on the pin location. As an example, imagine your golf ball is sitting in the fairway near a white post yardage marker. If the flag is red, then you should subtract yardage from the 150 yards to the center of the green suggested by the white yardage marker because you know the pin is in the front of the green. A blue flag will inform you to add yardage to a yardage marker. A white pin location will require no change to the yardage marker because it indicates the pin is in the center of the green, which is what the fairway yardage marker measures.

Having covered leadership at the practice area, it's now time to move to the next leadership moment in your golfing experience, the tee box. To get there, drive over with your special playing partner from the practice area to the tee box for the first hole.

Leadership at
the Tee Box

A golf course has five designated areas that are identified by the USGA and the R&A Golf Club, the governing bodies of golf. One designated area of the golf course is the teeing area, which contains the tee box where the first stroke on a hole is hit. A second designated area is the bunker area containing the sand traps where your ball might land if you hit a wayward shot. If the sand traps are in the fairway, they are referred to as fairway bunkers or fairway traps. Sand traps can also be near the green and are then often referred to as greenside traps. Special rules for playing when you are in a sand trap include that you are not allowed to let your golf club touch the sand before hitting the ball. You'll incur two penalty strokes if your club does touch the sand before being swung to hit the ball.

Another designated area of the golf course is the penalty area containing the water hazards and out of bounds areas for each hole. There are two types of water hazards referred to as lateral hazards and regular hazards. The difference between them is that a lateral water hazard is often located off to the side of the fairway or green while a regular water hazard is in the fairway or in front of the green. That's a simplified way to think about them but is helpful for visualizing where water hazards are located on the golf course.

The out of bounds area is also a part of the hazard area of a golf course. It is an area from which you cannot play your ball, and the boundaries are indicated by white stakes on the perimeter of a golf hole. These white stakes should not be confused with the white stakes in the fairway that serve as yardage markers indicating 150 yards from their location to the center of the green.

The next designated area on the golf course is the green, where the golf hole is located and where you putt the ball to end play on a hole. The green has special rules, which we will cover when we talk about leadership on the green. The final designated area is the general area, which refers to parts of the golf course not included in the previous four designated areas of teeing, bunkers, hazards, and green. For example, the fairway is part of the general area of the golf course.

In this chapter, we're going to discuss leadership in the teeing area when you're on the tee box waiting to hit your shot to start play on a hole. The USGA uses the technical term "teeing area" to describe the area at the beginning of each hole that has "a defined size and shape that is a two club-length deep rectangle measured from the tee markers you are playing your round from."[1] The tee markers come in pairs and are located on a raised area referred to as a tee box. A golfer can tee the ball up in the teeing area. The term "tee box" comes from the early history of the game, before the invention of the tee, when the golf course would provide a box containing wet sand at each teeing area. A golfer would grab a pinch of wet sand from the box and tee their ball on top of it in the teeing area. From that situation came the term "tee box" to represent the raised area containing the different teeing areas for a golf hole.

Fortunately, we no longer need actual tee boxes because of Dr. George Grant, who invented the wooden tee in 1899.[2] Dr. Grant was the child of parents who escaped from slavery. He became the second Black American to graduate from Harvard Dental School and was the first Black American to be a professor at Harvard.[3] Dr. Grant was a recreational golfer who invented the wooden tee when he played golf near his home in Arlington Heights, Illinois. For reasons that are unclear, Dr. Grant did not market his newly invented wooden golf tee, and thus, he did not financially benefit from his invention. It would take another thirty years before the first wooden tee was commercially offered by Dr. William Lowell from Maplewood, New Jersey, who also happened to be a dentist like Dr. Grant. While Dr. William was the first to commercialize the wooden tee, Dr. Grant is credited with being its inventor.[4]

The teeing area is located at the beginning of each hole and contains the tee box for the hole. The tee box is a closely mown area containing tee markers. There will always be a minimum of three tee markers that vary in their distance to the green on a hole, but they may be located on different tee boxes in the teeing area. According to USGA rules, you must tee the ball within a two club-length deep rectangle area behind the tee markers you are playing, and the tee must be inside the pair of tee markers. The USGA does allow your feet, but not the tee, to be outside of the tee markers. Within the tee markers, you have the option to tee the ball or place it on the ground and hit it. Let's now turn to discussing how you can be a leader at the tee box.

Empowerment

Showing leadership at the tee box starts with acting in an empowering manner, which means acting in a way that will enable you to perform best during the golfing experience from both playing and networking perspectives with your special playing partner. An important decision you will make that has implications for empowerment is which set of tee markers to play during the round. When you start to play your round on the first hole, you'll need to choose which set of tee markers on the tee box you will play and should use those markers on each hole as you go around the course. The four staple tee markers are colored black, blue, white, and red, respectively. The black tees are the furthest back in the teeing area and get played by people who hit far and tend to have a lower handicap. The distance to the green from the tee markers gets shorter as you move from the blue to the white to the red tee markers.

The choice of tee markers is important because it will determine the yardage or length of each hole on the course and the total yardage you will play during the round. In general, a shorter course is easier because you will need to hit fewer long shots, and this can be very helpful if you don't hit the ball well or are a beginner golfer. As a result, a shorter course is more likely to result in a positive golfing experience and give you more time to engage with your special playing partner because you will spend less time hitting shots, leaving you more time to talk with the people in your group.

Given that a shorter course is easier, why would anyone want to play anything but the forward tees at the front of the tee box? One reason is if they want to challenge their golfing skills by playing a longer version of the course. This is great for developing your golfing skills, but that's not why you're at the course if you're playing with a special playing partner. The golfing experience with a special playing partner is not the time to put your golf skills to the test. Your goal is to network, and playing the most challenging version of the course will take time and attention away from that goal. Playing a challenging version of a course is fine when the goal is to prepare for a competition or you're having a recreational round with your friends but not when you're on the course to network and access leadership opportunities.

Another reason people play the back tee markers rather than the forward tee markers is peer pressure. Everyone in the golf group does not have to play the same tee markers. That's the beauty of golf. You can play the course that best fits your game by choosing the tee markers that align best with your skill level. Yet you may feel like you should play the back markers if everyone in the group is playing them. Doing so will be a source of disempowerment if your skill level is not sufficient for playing the longer version of the course offered by the back tees. You'll end up finding yourself in hazards and struggling to get to the green. You're here to empower yourself and your special playing partner. Therefore, don't allow yourself to be pressured to play the back tees simply because

Practicing with the tee markers you plan to play is key to a successful round. Related to this, I was on the college golf team but far from one of the better players on the team. However, since it was my senior year, the coach decided that I would be one of the top five players from the team who would play in the conference championship tournament. Each school had five players, and I was number five on our team for this event. The tournament had players tee off by having the number five players from each team go first, followed by the number four players and so on until the best players tee off last. This meant that I would be the first player for our team to tee off, and I wanted to set a good example for my teammates and school. It also meant that I could be the first person to tee off and start the tournament if my name were called first.

Knowing this, I spent a good deal of time in the practice area before the round. I practiced hitting each club. I hit iron shots. I hit my woods. I hit chip shots and pitch shots. I practiced putting. However, the one thing that I practiced most was driving because I knew that I might have to start the tournament by driving in front of players from the ten schools in our conference and the coaches, assistant coaches, family, friends, and officials in attendance. I knew the drive was going to be important for me and my team and I spent time on the range practicing it. In the end, my name was called first and I did have to hit the opening tee shot in front of all those people. My practice paid off because my drive ended up in the fairway and set my round off to a good start.

—Eric

everyone else is playing them. Instead, comment to your playing partners, "The back tee markers are more than I'm ready to handle today," and that will generally be sufficient for them to accept your decision.

There are a couple of ways to determine which set of tee markers is best for you. One way is to look for the tee markers on a course that a professional male or female golfer might play and immediately eliminate them unless you consider yourself a professional golfer. The scorecard for every golf course will provide the aggregate yardage of the eighteen holes for each set of tee markers. The average length of a golf course on the men's professional golf tour, referred to as the PGA Tour, in the United States is 7,200 yards because they typically play from the black tee markers, which are farthest from the green on each hole.[5] Look for the set of tee markers that are this distance or greater and eliminate them from consideration. Professional women play on the LPGA Tour. The average length of a golf course during an LPGA tournament is 6,600 yards because they typically play from the blue or white tee markers. Again, eliminate any tee markers that will have you play a version of the course that is greater than the length of a course played by a professional unless you're as good as a professional golfer.

Another way to select tee markers for a round of golf is to base the decision on your handicap. We talked about the handicap system of golf when discussing leadership at the clubhouse. The front tees are generally for golfers with a high handicap, indicating that they typically shoot well above par for a round of golf. The back tee markers are appropriate for a low handicap golfer who typically shoots close to par because this golfer's skill level will allow them to best handle the challenges that come with playing a longer version of the golf course. According to the USGA, the average handicap for a male golfer is 14.2 and the average handicap for a female golfer is 27.5.[6] The more your handicap exceeds these averages, the more you should consider choosing one of the forward tee markers. Only choose the tee markers toward the back of the tee box if your handicap is lower than these averages.

A third way you can choose tee markers is to base the decision on how far you hit your driver. This option is recommended by the PGA, which published guidelines to help you make the choice.[7] These guidelines suggest that you should choose a set of tee markers with a total yardage under 7,000 yards unless you can drive the ball 300 yards. If you drive the ball 200 yards, then choose a set of tee markers that is between 5,200 and 5,400 yards in length. You'll need to have a sense of how far you drive the ball to use these numbers and can use your time in the practice area to determine how far you typically drive the golf ball. Once you have that information, follow the PGA's recommendations to select a set of tee markers that will be empowering at the tee box.

There is also one final point to make about choosing tee markers that will empower you. It's not only about empowering yourself to have a positive golfing experience with your playing partner. It's also about empowering yourself to make a good impression. Choosing to play a set of tee markers that results in you not playing well and taking time away from interacting with your special playing partner is not going to leave the impression that you're a leader. If you play the back tees on the course, several potentially bad things are going to happen. First, your special playing partner will think you're a highly skilled golfer, but that perception is going to go away quickly once they see you struggling on every hole because you're playing a set of tee markers beyond your golf skill. This will result in your special playing partner wondering if you are just trying to impress them and whether you are someone whose decision-making is to be trusted. Second, by playing the back tees, your special playing partner might feel pressured to join you in playing a longer and more challenging version of the golf course than they may be ready for or capable of playing. If they succumb to this pressure, they are likely to struggle and focus on their golf game rather than interacting with you in a positive manner that will nurture the relationship between the two of you. Remember, the golfing experience is a step toward networking with your special playing partner. Be sure you are sending the right signals to them about the type of leader you are and what they can expect in a relationship with you.

Integrity

Integrity is also important at the tee box and requires that you be respectful. The choice of tee markers discussed earlier can be a moment requiring integrity. For instance, many people may use the terms "men's tees" and "ladies' tees" when describing which tee markers they're playing or when asking others which tees they plan to play. It's not uncommon to hear a male golfer say, "I'm playing the men's tees" or ask a woman if she's playing the ladies' tees at the tee box of the first hole. When it's used, "ladies' tees" always refers to the frontmost set of tee markers, which are always red. If you're a woman, you may be asked whether you're playing the red tees.

This type of language is a form of microaggression because it implicitly questions the ability of women to play a longer version of the course. It segregates the tee box, putting women at the front and men at any of the remaining tee markers on the tee box. Let's be clear. Red is not a gender, and women can play any set of tee markers they wish, so you shouldn't feel compelled to play the forward tees if you're a woman. If you are a woman golfer and not planning to play the red tees, you might respond when someone asks you if you're playing the ladies' tees by saying, "No, are you?" as a way of making the microaggression visible to the perpetrator. Or you might respond by saying, "I'm playing the white tees" if someone asks if you're playing the ladies tees at the tee box.

Fortunately, this form of language on the tee box is becoming less popular, as illustrated by a recent experience of our daughter on the golf course. At the first tee, the starter checked her in and proceeded to ask, "Are you playing the re—" before catching himself and saying that he understood that type of language was not respectful before apologizing. He then proceeded to ask her the more respectful question, "Which set of tees are you playing today?" She told him and started the round.

Another time when integrity is called for at the tee box concerns ensuring the tee box remains a point of community and not division. This is important to remember because of the unique nature of the tee box. It is one of the few places on the golf course where all golfers in a group come together to hit the ball. This makes it an important point of community where small talk and brief conversations take place among golfers in a group. However, the potential for division at the tee box arises if people in the group are playing different tee markers. Let's say that you're playing the back tees and your special playing partner is playing the front tees. These two sets of tee markers can be very far apart on the tee box and may even be on different tee boxes. There can be a tendency for you to stand by your tee markers at the back of the teeing area and your special playing partner to stand toward the front of the teeing area near their tee markers. This is bad and disrespectful for several reasons. First, your special playing partner could be hit if you hit a wayward drive. Second, you are not being respectful and supporting each other on the tee. You need your special playing partner to help you track an errant shot and vice versa, but staying apart in the teeing area hampers both of you in this regard. Third, you or your special playing partner can be left out of important small talk and conversations on the tee box. This can happen if there are other golfers in your group, all of whom are playing the same tee markers except for you or your special playing partner.

Instead of being apart, you should stand near your special playing partner and vice versa when each of you is hitting your shot from the tee box. If you're playing one of the back tees, invite your special playing partner to join you if they are playing one of the forward tee markers. The same applies if you're playing the front tees and your special playing partner is playing one of the back tees. This approach is more respectful, and it will enable you to better use the time at the tee box for networking. There's often a lot of opportunity for small talk on the tee box, especially if you're waiting for the group in front of you to hit their shots from the fairway. Remember, you're out there to network. You want to be constantly engaging in conversation with the people in your playing group, especially your special playing partner. You can't do that if the two of you are in separate areas of the teeing area.

Another issue requiring integrity at the tee box is the order of play. There is a process for determining the order of play for a group of golfers in the teeing area. If you're on the first hole and people are playing different tee markers, the person playing the tee markers furthest back would go first and then the order of play would follow the tee markers and the people playing them moving toward the front of the tee box. For instance, a tee box may have three sets of tee markers with black being in the back, white in the middle, and red in the front. Anyone hitting from the black tees would hit first, followed by anyone hitting from the white tees, followed by the golfers hitting from the red tees.

When not on the first hole, the order of golfers hitting from the same tee markers is determined by their score on previous holes, with the golfer who had the best score on the previous hole hitting first. If there is a tie for best score on the previous hole, the scores on the next hole back are compared and the process continues until one golfer is determined to have had the best score. Let's illustrate this with an example. Mike and Jasmine are on the tee box at the fifth hole and are both hitting from the same tee markers. Jasmine would hit first on the tee box if her score was better than Mike's on the fourth hole, and Mike would hit first if he had the better score on that hole. If they tied on the fourth hole, they would compare their scores on the third hole, and the person with the lowest score would hit first. Let's say they tied on the third hole. Then they compare their scores on the second hole and so forth until one of them has the better score.

On the first tee, there are no previous scores to compare. In that case, someone can volunteer to go first, or a more common way to decide is to toss a golf tee in their air and let it land on the ground. Whomever it points to will go first. You then toss it in the air again and let it land among the remaining golfers. Again, whomever it points to will go next, and the process continues until an order of play is assigned for all the golfers to start the round at the first tee. Alternatively, you may hear someone in the group say, "Let's just play ready golf," which means that the order will be determined by whoever is ready to hit first and then proceeds accordingly. This way of ordering is common if you're more concerned about the pace of play than following the honor system. The easiest way to determine which you should follow is to ask the people in your group by saying something like, "Are we following the honor system on the tee or playing ready golf today?"

Mindfulness

"People will stare at me when I'm on the tee," said Annabel Dimmock, a professional golfer on the Ladies European Tour.[8] According to Dimmock, people stare when she's about to hit at the tee box because they question the appropriateness of the clothing she wears and whether she should be on the golf course as a woman and as a woman wearing her style of fashion. The unwelcome stares quickly fade once they see her hit the ball.

Having people casually watch you while you hit from the tee box is expected because they are waiting for their turn to hit and are prepared to help you track your ball once you hit it. However, being stared at is different, and it can create problems for your ability to have a good golfing experience with your special playing partner. A woman can experience an objectifying stare or gaze on a golf course when a man focuses his attention on her appearance rather than her playing. For example, former professional golfer Paige Renee Spiranac has described how she sometimes encounters situations in which men use range finders to stare at her from across the course.[9] Women are not the only people who get stared at while they're on the golf course. A Black man on the golf course may experience other golfers staring at him because he is a Black man playing a sport in which 97 percent of players are white.[10]

The effect of being stared at can have an impact, as research has shown that those experiencing an unwelcome stare perform worse on a task compared with those not experiencing an unwelcome stare, and the negative impact can be greater for women than men.[11] The negative impact occurs because the stare causes the person experiencing it to begin questioning why they are being stared at, leading them to form doubts about their ability, or even worse, it may cause them to doubt whether they belong. As a result, a person's confidence can fall, resulting in poor performance, physical stress, and other negative consequences when receiving an unwelcome stare.[12] Any one of these effects can potentially prevent you from having a successful golfing experience with your special playing partner.

One way to combat the negative experiences that a stare can promote is by acting with mindfulness in this type of situation. The positive effect of mindfulness is related to research showing that your ability to successfully manage the self-questioning and self-doubt that can accompany the experience of being stared at depends upon your approach to the experience. Individuals who can accept the uncertainty of knowing exactly why someone is staring at them and respond in a more intentional manner are more willing to act in a nonconforming manner and are less likely to question themselves.[13] When not practicing mindfulness, people experiencing an unwelcome stare tend to start the negative thinking cycle of self-questioning and self-doubt, which can be persistent, resulting in negative consequences. Why is mindfulness so effective in this situation? Research has shown that mindfulness is beneficial because it promotes the types of mental reactions necessary to prevent the negative thinking patterns that are the source of the negative reactions.[14]

Being mindful means recognizing what is happening in the present moment and not getting distracted by replays of what has happened in the past or rehearsals of what is expected or hoped for in the future. By being mindful at the tee box when experiencing an unwelcome stare, you'll be able to quickly recognize any negative changes in your mood and thinking that may be reactions to the stare. You are thus better able to examine in a nonjudgmental manner what you are experiencing because of the stare. This puts you into a better position to choose whether to continue down a path of negative thinking or change to a different, more positive perspective focused on making your best shot in that moment.

You can practice mindfulness in these situations in several ways. One way is to observe in a nonjudgmental manner what is happening in the moment, including the stare but also the actions and words of others around you. Often, others will not be staring at you and may even not be paying any attention to you. This allows you to engage in the next step of the mindfulness process, which is awareness of the entire situation at that moment so that you can understand that the perpetrator's actions are an isolated action by one person who is just a small part of everything else happening at that moment. This enables you to accept the action without judgment and see the stare as a small part of the entire landscape of experiences occurring at the tee box. This process of mindfulness should leave you able to prevent self-questioning and self-doubt from creeping into and taking control of your thinking process at the tee box.

You can get distracted by anything on a golf course. Since it is always relatively quiet, you can get startled easily, for example by wind picking up in the trees or an animal crossing the fairway. Being mindful will enable you to shift to focusing on hitting your tee shot the best that you can and not letting the quiet nature of golf or an unwelcome stare tarnish your golfing experience and prevent you from networking with your special playing partner.

Curiosity

When you're acting with curiosity at the tee box, you're obtaining knowledge that will help you make good decisions about what shot you want to hit and take the actions required to make it happen. A helpful source of knowledge at the tee box is the tee box signage. On most golf courses, there will be some type of signage that will provide information about the hole. This information will help you decide the strategy you want to play on the hole and the shot you need to hit at the tee box.

The information on the tee signage will vary from golf course to golf course. The first piece of information to search for on the tee signage is the par score for the hole. Is the hole a par 3, par 4, or par 5? If it's a par 3, you know immediately that you'll be trying to land your shot from the tee box on the green. Alternatively, a par 5 will require at least one and more likely two shots from the fairway before you hit onto the green. This information will be very helpful in setting a strategy for a hole.

The tee signage will also provide the yardage for each set of tee markers on the hole. There are no set rules establishing the maximum or minimum length for a par 3, par 4, or par 5 hole. However, the USGA does provide guidelines for hole length.[15] It suggests a par 3 hole be no longer than 260 yards. The recommended range for a par 4 is between 240 and 490 yards, and for a par 5, the range is 370 to 710 yards. The tee signage will provide you with the actual yardage for the hole and will help you select the club you want to hit from the tee box. If the golf hole is long, you can choose a club like the driver, which is the club that can hit the ball the farthest because of its design, having the longest shaft and one of the lowest clubface angles of any club. Alternatively, the yardage may suggest the need for less distance. If you have another club that you feel more comfortable hitting off the tee, you can use that as well. The driver is not everyone's favorite club, or you may only have up to a 3 wood in your bag. Being curious at the tee box and using the tee signage to know the yardage for a hole will help you make these types of decisions.

Another piece of information to look for on the tee signage is the designated areas of the hole. Where are the bunkers and hazard areas that you want to avoid? Good tee signage will indicate where these areas are on the golf hole. For example, you'll be able to tell if there are fairway bunkers that you need to avoid on your drive. Alternatively, maybe there are only bunkers around the green. Likewise, use the tee signage to identify the presence and location of water hazards and out of bounds areas. The best tee signage will also show the contour or outline of the different designated areas of a hole. This additional information is very helpful because it gives you a sense of the size of these areas so you can better plan your shot from the tee box. By being curious and using the tee signage to locate the designated areas on a golf hole, you can gain the knowledge needed to avoid the penalties that come with hitting into hazards and the challenges that come from playing out of the bunkers.

It is not common, but some golf courses or golf holes do not have tee signage. In that case, check the scorecard. Many times, the golf course will provide a visual layout of each hole on the scorecard. The visual layout on the score card is helpful, but it often lacks the detail that can be found on the tee signage. In the best-case scenario, you will be provided with both and can act curiously at the tee box using both the score card and tee box signage to gather hole information.

Your curiosity when considering the tee box signage should also focus on the layout of the golf hole you are about to play. Not all golf holes are straight. Golf architects usually build some form of bend in many of the holes on a golf course. The history of golf architecture is a long one, going back to the early days of golf's beginnings in Scotland. Some of the more well-known golf architects include Old Tom Morris, Willie Park Jr., Harry Colt, Donald Ross, Tom Doak, and Pete Dye.[16] A less known but equally important golf architect is Joseph M. Bartholomew, who was the first Black golf architect in the United States. His story is one filled with both accomplishment and sadness. Born in 1885 in New Orleans, his accomplishments were numerous and included building many public and private golf courses in New Orleans and the surrounding area. However, because of segregation at the time, he was never able to play any of the golf courses he designed. He did build and own several golf courses that he used to earn his living and provide Black people with access to golf. In 1972, his achievements were recognized by the City of New Orleans with his induction into the Greater New Orleans Sports Hall of Fame.[17]

When golf architects design some form of bend in a golf hole, they will have the hole bend either to the right or left. Where that bend occurs can vary. It may bend early in the hole and close to the tee box. It may bend in the middle of the fairway, or it may bend closer to the green. The bend can be slight or severe. The direction of the bend is described using the term "dogleg" and whether it bends to the right ("dogleg right") or left ("dogleg left"). Why is the term "dogleg" used? There is no scientific reason for the term's use. One thought is that a bending hole mimics the shape of a dog's back legs.

Strategy

Once you exercise your curiosity on the tee box, you're ready to be strategic with your shot and with networking. We'll start with being strategic with your shot from the tee box, which involves deciding how to play the golf hole in front of you. Your goal on a par 3 is to hit the ball from the tee box onto the green and then take two putts to earn your par. You'll want to avoid the hazards you identified from your curiosity, and doing so may require a certain type of shot. For example, imagine there is a water hazard in front of the green. Hitting onto the green will require you to fly the ball all the way to the green to avoid the water. The strategy might be different without the presence of the hazard because then you could also consider hitting a lower shot that lands short of the green and rolls or bounces on.

Strategizing your play on a par 3 hole requires focusing primarily on the green. The strategizing gets more complicated when you're standing at the tee box of a par 4 or par 5 hole because you must combine multiple shots together into a strategy. On a par 4 hole, for instance, you need to think about where to try to land the ball in the fairway so that you have an easier shot onto the green. A par 5 is even more complex strategically because you must plan three shots in making your way to the green: the drive into the fairway, the shot down the fairway, and the shot from the fairway onto the green. A good goal for your strategy in both cases is to land the ball in the fairway.

However, landing in the fairway may require you to make certain choices about your aim, where you hit from at the tee box, and which club you choose. Imagine you're standing at the tee box on a par 4. Your curiosity used the tee signage to identify a fairway bunker on the left. In this case, you will want to aim toward the right side of the fairway to avoid the fairway bunker. To help you aim to the right, you could hit from the left side of the area between the tee markers because this will allow you to aim away from the fairway bunker as you position yourself to hit the ball toward the right side of the fairway.

Maybe you're concerned about being able to hit the ball toward the right side of the fairway. This might be the case if you hit a draw or occasionally hook the golf ball, resulting in a ball flight that goes from right to left as it travels in the air and down the fairway. You may know that the fairway bunker is 200 yards away from the tee box. If you're not confident about hitting the ball to the right side of the fairway, you might choose to hit your drive from the tee box with a club that will not send the ball more than 200 yards down the fairway. In this situation, your aim, hitting position between the tee markers, and club selection are all based on giving you the best chance to avoid the fairway bunker and land in the fairway. If you are a new player, you may not know how to do this on command. This is where your practice on the range will come in handy. Learning to recognize the kind of path your ball trajectory follows will help you in the decision-making process of where to aim. Practice makes perfect!

The point of this strategizing is that you want to play shots that will put you into a good position to hit your shots from the fairway onto the green. Doing so has several advantages. First, you will score better. Second, your pace of play will be good. Each benefit will help you play well. Yet you're also at the golf course to network and create opportunities for advancing your professional career. The third reason for strategizing on the tee addresses networking goals that are important at the tee box because you will signal your ability to be strategic to your special playing partner by using the information you gained through curiosity to strategically choose an aiming point in the fairway, a position to hit from between the tee markers, and a club to hit at each tee box. This could be an important signal to send if your special playing partner is someone senior in your company who may be looking for someone to promote into a strategic leadership position. It also could be important with a potential customer who wants to work with a supplier who can help them strategize.

Strategically playing at the tee box will also provide another benefit for networking. It will provide material for engaging in small talk with your playing partner during the round. Let's say that you aimed down the left side of the fairway so you could hit your driver from the tee box to avoid a water hazard on the right side of the fairway. You then successfully hit the shot, leaving your ball sitting on the left side of the fairway. Everyone knows that hitting the shot you want is difficult in golf. You might say something like, "Wow, this game is so enjoyable when the ball goes where I aim it. If I could just have that happen more often, it would be even more fun" to your special playing partner. All golfers know the challenge but also the invigoration that comes from hitting a shot that follows what you planned to happen. Your special playing partner is very likely to agree with your statement and add something like, "Yeah, isn't that the truth. Wish that happened more for me too." You've just used your strategizing at the tee box to create a sense of shared interest with your special playing partner by bringing out in your small talk that you both appreciate the challenge and delight associated with planning and executing a good golf shot at the tee box. Bringing out similarities between you and your special playing partner is key to developing rapport and trust between the two of you.[18] All golfers must choose a club, choose a spot to hit from, and aim from the tee box. Strategizing around these decisions and using them for small talk will help you bring the similarities between you and your special playing partner into your conversation, allowing you to be more successful in using the golfing experience for achieving your networking goals.

Adaptability

Adaptability is also important at the tee box in several situations. The format of play you are following can require you to adapt frequently at the tee box. A very common format is stroke play, which involves playing your ball throughout the entire round, resulting in an individual score for each player at the end of the round based on the number of strokes required to play all the golf holes. However, you may play a team format that involves each person hitting from the tee box. Rather than having everyone hit their next shot from where their individual drive landed, each person will hit from the location of the best drive from among the drives hit by the group from the tee box. This process of hitting based on the location of the best shot from the group of golfers continues throughout the round and is called by several names, including "scramble" and "captain's choice." If you are playing this team format, you will likely be required to adapt your shot at the tee box based on the shots of the people in your playing group.

Imagine, for instance, that you are playing a best ball format with three other people in your playing group. The first three golfers hit their drives from the tee box and none of them landed in the fairway. One landed in a water hazard. One ended up in a fairway bunker, and one is out of bounds. None of these balls presents the team with a good situation for hitting the next shot. The team needs a drive in the fairway to make the next shot easier. Your typical approach may be to hit a driver because the hole is a long par 4 and you want to make the second shot as short as possible so that it is easier to hit it onto the green with the second shot. Going for distance often requires sacrificing control. With the shots of your teammates in trouble, it may be better for the team if you use a club that may not hit long but will have a higher likelihood of having your ball land in the fairway.

Adapting in this manner when you're playing a team format will help your team score better for the round. It will also send a strong signal to those in your playing group like your special playing partner that you are a team player. You could have followed your typical play and tried to hit the longest drive you could on the hole, but that would not have taken the rest of the team into consideration. Being a team golfer is considered a characteristic of an individual who is further along in the development of their leadership ability.[19] By adapting to the situation and showing you are a team player in the process, the tee box becomes a place where you can display your leadership ability to your special playing partner.

Hitting from the tee box may also require adapting your drive based on your skill level. Let's say the golf hole you are about to play is a long par 3, and we mean very long. Do you take a club that allows you to hit the ball the farthest and just swing away? This is the situation that faced Billy Casper in the 1959 US Open. Hole 3 on the golf course was a very long par 3, measuring 216 yards. While many of today's par 3s measure longer than that, the yardage was very long in 1959 for a par 3. Casper made a double bogey playing hole 3 during a practice round before the tournament. The long yardage made it difficult for him to land the ball on the green from the tee box, and the sand traps surrounding the green, combined with a very hilly green on which the ball rolled quickly, made it daunting to make a par 3 if you missed the green. This led Casper to hit his 5 iron and have the ball land short of the green (also known as a "layup") rather than trying to hit a longer iron onto the green and run the risk of missing the green in one of the sand traps. This adaptation meant that Casper had to chip onto the green and make the putt in one stroke to par hole 3. Putting was his strength, though, and this adaptation played to his strength. As he described it, "I felt if you hit the ball right or left, it wasn't that easy to make a bogey on the hole. I felt you were setting yourself up for at least a bogey or a double bogey. I watched some of my competitors do it."[20] Casper's approach was unorthodox. Most golfers in the tournament tried to hit the green from the tee box on hole 3. By adapting his play to his strengths, Casper managed to par hole 3 on each of the four days of the tournament and ended up winning the tournament by one stroke. The best golfer is often the smartest player on the course. Sometimes choosing unorthodox approaches can prevent you from shooting a larger number all around.

The point in this case is that sometimes the adaptations you need to make may require playing a shot or playing a hole in an atypical fashion. Casper's victory illustrates the success that is possible when you do so. For him, it meant winning a major golf tournament. For you, it will mean adapting your play in a way that puts you in the best position to play well and have an enjoyable experience with your special playing partner. It will also signal to your playing partner your willingness to be innovative in how you approach a challenge and will likely provide a great topic for small talk during and after the round. Each of these benefits will contribute to your success in the golfing experience.

Being a leader at the tee box is not easy. However, being empowering, mindful, curious, strategic, and adaptable and acting with integrity will enable you to effectively manage the leadership challenges presented at the tee box. Now, let's turn to discussing how these same traits will help you be a leader in the fairway.

Leadership in
the Fairway

The fairway lies in the defined area of the golf course that runs from the tee box to the green. What makes the fairway unique from other defined areas is that it is the closely mown area on a golf hole into which you hit your ball from the tee box and from which you hit your ball toward the green. Not all golf holes have a fairway. Par 4s and par 5s have a fairway that you attempt to hit into from the tee box and then hit from toward the green. Par 3s do not have a fairway to hit into per se because you are trying to hit the ball from the tee box onto the green. Unless you're playing an island green that is surrounded by water, there will be a closely mown area running from the tee box to the green on a par 3, but it's not common to hear someone refer to this area as a fairway unless the golf course has designated it as such.

One of the important aspects of the fairway from a playing perspective is that the rules of golf require you to play the ball as it lies once you hit it from the tee box. This means that you cannot touch the ball regardless of where it lies after you hit your drive without taking a penalty stroke. One exception occurs if your ball stops on the cart path. In that case, you get a free drop within two club lengths of the cart path but no closer to the hole. Another exception is when the course is very wet and the golf course allows players to lift, clean, and place their ball if it is sitting in water in the fairway. The phrase "lift, clean, and place" means that you can lift the ball from where it sits in the fairway, clean it, and then place it back in the fairway in a dry area as close as possible to where it was originally lying and no closer to the hole. The pro shop will tell you if this is the case when you check in. Otherwise, you must play the ball as it lies in the fairway.

The closely mown grass of the fairway provides the best area to hit from compared with the other defined areas like the hazards and bunkers. Other parts of the general area include the trees and the rough, where the grass has been allowed to grow to varying lengths by the golf course. Hitting from the trees is difficult because you may be blocked from hitting the ball forward by the trunk of a tree, or the canopy of a tree may prevent you from hitting up and over the trees toward the green. The grass in some areas of the rough can be so tall that it is difficult to find your ball or to hit it once you do find it. You will not face any of these challenges hitting from the fairway. It is unlikely there will be trees in your way, and the closely mown area allows you to easily find and hit your ball.

The fairway is also important from a networking perspective. The fairway is where you will spend most of the golfing experience with your special playing partner because it is where you spend most of your time as you make your way around the golf course. You can ride in a golf cart, or some courses allow you to either carry your bag or use a wheeled pushcart and walk the golf course. Doing so is great exercise and can provide opportunities while you're walking to engage in small talk with your special playing partner. In the riding cart, most of your time will be spent driving from the tee box into the fairway to find and hit your ball and the ball of your special playing partner. It will also be spent driving from the fairway to the green area to play your shots around and on the green.

Some of the extensive time you spend in the fairway with your special playing partner will be filled with promise as you both stand over your balls in the fairway with hopes of hitting a great shot to the green. On other occasions, your time in the fairway may involve disappointment as you watch your respective shots from the fairway not go exactly where you had planned. Another emotion that you may experience is frustration as you make your way down the fairway to find that your ball or that of your special playing partner has landed in a fairway bunker, hazard, or one of the less desirable general areas like the woods or rough that surround the fairway.

The mix of emotions that will be a part of the golfing experience with your special playing partner during your time in the fairway will present both opportunities and threats to the networking opportunity. For instance, watching as your special playing partner hits a shot from the fairway onto the green and close to the hole will create a positive shared experience that can be a source of congratulations, small talk, and positive shared memories that will help in developing a relationship between the two of you.[1] However, a poorly hit shot from the fairway by your special playing partner can cause them anxiety, lead them to stop talking, and create a negative shared experience. Any of these experiences will make relationship building difficult. These situations may also result from your actions. You may cause a positive shared experience through a great shot from the fairway or a negative shared experience through a poor shot and a negative reaction to it like throwing a golf club in frustration. Regardless of the source, your time in the fairway is filled with opportunities and threats to the golfing experience, and success from both a playing and networking perspective requires leadership. Let's now turn to discussing the type of leadership that is required in the fairway.

Strategy

Strategy in the fairway from a playing perspective involves deciding what shot to hit. On a par 4 hole, that decision involves where to try to land the ball onto the green so that you will have an easier opportunity to birdie or par the hole, depending on whether it takes you one or two putts on the green. One way to try to reach this goal is to hit the ball toward the flag on the green with the intention of having it stop near the hole. However, there can be cases where you need to aim away from the hole to ensure you land on the green and leave yourself with a makeable putt. For instance, imagine you're on the left side of the fairway and the flag is on the left side of the green. Located left of the green is a sand trap. There is a lot of room to the right of the pin since it is tucked on the left side of the green. There are also no bunkers on the right side. Do you hit straight for the pin and try to fly over the sand trap on the left side with the hope that the ball will clear the sand trap and stop near the hole? Or do you aim to the right of the hole and take the sand trap on the left out of play but potentially leave yourself with a longer putt? The scenario you just imagined involves course management, which refers to deciding how best to play a shot from the fairway toward the green. It is a very crucial part of being a good golfer. The smart play in this case is to take the bunker out of play by aiming to the right of the green because doing so increases the odds that your ball will land on the green, leaving you with a makeable putt.

A similar situation can arise on a par 5 hole. Let's imagine you are standing over your drive in the fairway deciding if you will try to hit the ball onto the green with your second shot or hit a layup shot that leaves you short of the green with an easy shot to hit onto the green. Let's add to the scenario a water hazard just in front of the green. To use a common golfing term, do you "go for it" with your second shot, meaning you're going to try to avoid the water hazard and land the ball on the green with a long shot from the fairway? It is important to recall in this type of situation that your goal for the golfing experience is to network and not to score your best round. If the latter happens without you planning for it, then great. Given your networking goal, the smarter play from the fairway is to hit the shot that will leave you more time to spend conversing with your special playing partner and will create a positive experience for you both. Trust us when we say this: it will not be a positive experience for anyone in the group if you're constantly having to take extra strokes or losing balls in the hazards.

What will be much more of an influence on the outcome of the golfing experience than your score is how enjoyable you are to spend time with during the four or more hours it will take to play an eighteen-hole round of golf. A great deal of this time will be spent in the fairway with your special playing partner. One goal that will help make your time in the fairway a positive experience is to use the fairway time to reduce the social distance between you and your special playing partner. Unless you and your special playing partner are close friends, there will be some level of distance or lack of social closeness. Some of the social distance could exist because your special playing partner may be a manager or a top leader at your current employer and the difference in rank creates social distance. The same could be true if your special playing partner is a high-ranking individual at another firm. Demographic differences like race and nationality can also create social distance that can make developing a strong relationship challenging during your time in the fairway.[2]

It is important that you lessen this distance by using small talk. One way to accomplish this goal is to promote frequent and casual discussions through self-disclosure about topics you feel comfortable sharing with your special playing partner.[3] An important distinction should be made, however, about the nature of self-disclosure that is more effective in socially distant situations. Sharing information that confirms the social distance between you and your special playing partner will be counterproductive and only reinforce the distance between the two of you.[4] For example, sharing information about your children with a special playing partner who does not have children can highlight the differences between you and them. Instead, share information that highlights what you and your special playing partner have in common, and the social distance between you will start to lessen. You can talk about where you went to college, for instance, if your special playing partner also attended college or, even better, if they went to the same college as you. This type of self-disclosure has a greater chance of nurturing a stronger relationship between the two of you.

The emotions you show in the fairway will also impact social closeness. Showing gratitude when your special playing partner compliments one of your shots to the green or helps you find a drive that ended up in the rough can also lessen social distance.[5] Being compassionate when your special playing partner plays a poor shot can also help reduce social distance. Each of these actions will

help build closeness by revealing similarities between the two of you and showing that you are not acting solely on your own behalf but also value your special
playing partner's experiences.

We'll illustrate with an example. Imagine that your special playing partner
is the CEO of your current employer and you've invited them out because you're
interested in learning more about an open position that was just posted by human
resources. The position would be a promotion into a leadership role but would
require you to move from your current area to a new area in the firm. Also imagine that the CEO is not from the same country as you and is much older. There
are at least three sources of social distance in this scenario. The person is higher
ranked in the firm, has a different nationality, and is older than you. Working in
your favor to decrease the social distance is that you both work at the same firm.
Early in the round, you should casually reveal pieces of information about yourself like where you went to school or why you play golf. This self-disclosure will
in turn prompt self-disclosure by your special playing partner in related areas,
providing opportunities for the recognition of similarities between the two of you
that is critical to developing a closer, more trusting relationship.[6] You should also
look for opportunities to compliment your special playing partner when they
make a good shot, but don't compliment every shot because doing so can lead to
suspicion about your motives.[7] You should also thank your special playing partner when they help you in different ways like finding a yardage marker in the
fairway or locating the pin on the green. These actions individually and in combination will help reduce the social distance between you and a special playing
partner, allowing for a closer relationship to form and providing you with better
access to leadership.

Curiosity

Acting with curiosity in the fairway contributes to building a closer relationship
with your special playing partner. In addition to sharing information about
yourself and offering gratitude and compassion when appropriate, you should
also ask questions of your special playing partner that provide an opportunity
for them to share things about themselves that they feel comfortable disclosing.
It's important to keep in mind that the fairway is not the place where your questions should focus on business or whatever professional goal motivated you to
invite the special playing partner to play a round of golf with you. The time

between shots is too short for the type of in-depth discussion required to support these goals.

Using small talk to effectively develop a relationship with your special playing partner requires both focusing on the right topics and doing so in the right manner over the course of the entire round, much of which will be spent in the fairway. The topics should provide for personal self-disclosure, they should advance to escalating levels of self-disclosure over time, and you should reciprocate with your answers to the questions.[8] To illustrate, imagine the round as three sets of six holes rather than one round of eighteen holes. This gives us set 1 as holes 1 through 6, set 2 as holes 7 through 12, and set 3 as holes 13 through 18. The questions you ask in the fairways of the holes in set 1 should allow for self-disclosure of your special playing partner about their personal values. For example, you could ask them how they would describe their perfect day on the golf course or ask them whom they would play a round of golf with if they could invite anyone in the world. Likewise, you should share your answers to the same questions.

The nature of the topics you ask about should change as you get to set 2, consisting of holes 7 through 12. To support escalating self-disclosure, ask questions about the special playing partner and their relationships with others. Questions like "Does everyone in your family play golf?" and "Where do you and your family usually go on vacation?" escalate the nature of the disclosure because they are asking not only about your special playing partner but also other people who are personally important to them. The questions should escalate even further as you get to holes 13 through 18 in set 3 because you should then ask questions that involve self-disclosure relative to the two of you. To do this, you can comment to your partner that you're working on a part of your game and ask them to watch you hit the ball and give you feedback relative to what you're working on. You may be working, for example, on keeping your head still during your putting stroke and can ask your partner to watch and let you know if you're staying still. Be sure to ask about something you are working on where you could use their help. Otherwise, it will come across as disingenuous. You can also make "we" statements later in the round that can elicit self-disclosure from your special playing partner about you, like "We should do this again" if the round is going extremely well.

Asking the right types of questions at the appropriate times takes practice. It will help to prepare questions for the earlier, middle, and later holes in the round that provide for the type of self-disclosure necessary for nurturing the relationship between you and your special playing partner. You'll also need to be a good listener, watching and listening for the types of responses that signal the social distance between the two of you is falling. These include the details your special playing partner provides in answering questions and whether they ask you questions that provide an opportunity for your self-disclosure. The more your special playing partner self-discloses, the more trust they have in you and the closer your relationship with them is.[9]

Although using your curiosity to develop the relationship with your special playing partner is important, you also need to use your curiosity in the fairway to help you play well. You are likely to have the ball sitting up nicely for you to hit if it is in the fairway. Yet to play the shot well, you will need to collect additional information. First, you should determine the yardage of the shot you are about to play. Some people carry a range finder that they use to get an exact measurement of the yardage. The range finder uses GPS and simply requires you to point at the target and click. If you don't have a range finder, you should find the yardage marker closest to your ball in the fairway and count off how many steps you are from the marker. Subtract the number of steps from the yardage for the marker if you are in front of the marker or add them if you're behind the marker.

You should also use your curiosity to learn about the wind. The ball is going to fly through the air once you hit it, and the flight can be impacted by the wind. The wind may be blowing from behind you toward your target, which is known as a tailwind. This type of wind will add yardage to the shot because it will carry the ball forward in the air. The wind could be a headwind, meaning that the wind is blowing toward you from the target. A headwind will reduce the yardage of the shot because it will push against the ball as it flies. Crosswinds occur when the wind is blowing from right to left or vice versa. These winds won't affect distance but can impact the direction the ball flies in the air. There is no one method for determining the impact of wind, but a suggested rule of thumb is to drop 1 yard from the typical distance you hit a club for every mile per hour of headwind you're hitting into and add 1 yard for every mile per hour of tailwind.[10]

You will also want to be curious about the angle of the lie for your ball in the fairway. The ball may be lying on a downhill slope in the fairway. If so, the ball will typically fly lower and farther when you hit it. Another possibility is that the golf ball will be lying on an angle sloping uphill. The ball will go higher when hit from an upslope and typically travel less distance than if you hit from level ground in the fairway. The ball also may be lying above or below your feet in the fairway.[11] Hitting a ball lying above your feet will cause the ball to move left in the air. The opposite is true when hitting a ball lying below your feet. It will most likely fly to the right in the air.

Information about the yardage, wind, and lie is important to collect when you're in the fairway. The yardage will tell you how far you need to hit the ball, and this will help you select the right club to hit. The lie will help you understand the flight of the ball, which will help you determine the aim for your shot. The wind can impact yardage, direction, or both, influencing potentially both the club selected and the aim of the shot played from the fairway. However, not all shots from the tee box end up in the fairway. When they don't, you must adapt.

Adaptability

An important point to remember is that you are very, very unlikely to hit the fairway with every drive. Consider the statistics of professional golfers as proof. Recent statistics indicate that the average percentage of drives landing in the fairway from female professionals on the LPGA Tour is 72 percent, and the percentage falls to 60 percent when you consider the drives from male professionals playing on the PGA Tour.[12] If professional golfers don't always hit the fairway, then you shouldn't expect to either. Instead, you should be ready to adapt to where your drive does end up. Some of the more likely places include the rough, the fairway bunkers, and the trees. Each landing spot will require you to adapt your shot accordingly.

Landing in the rough means that your ball lies in the tall unmown grass that surrounds the fairway. How you play from the rough depends on the height of the grass. The rough can be only slightly taller than the mown grass in the fairway. In this case, the rough is considered "light rough," and playing from this type of rough requires you to play very similarly to how you would play the ball from the fairway but with one exception. Hitting the ball from grass that is slightly higher than the grass in the fairway can result in the ball flying farther than normal for a club. This type of effect is referred to as a "flyer" and occurs because grass gets between the clubface and the ball when you contact the ball in the light rough, reducing the spin of the ball and causing it to fly further and roll further after it lands.[13] The key adaptation required in the light rough is to account for the extra distance you are likely to get by using a club with which you may not typically be able to hit the distance you need for the shot. The potential for a flyer means that the club will likely hit the ball farther, making up for choosing a club that usually does not fly the distance you need.

The length of the grass will increase as you move away from the fairway into the rough. The area with the longest grass is called the "deep rough" because of how far below the top of the grass the ball lies. The challenge in the deep rough is to get the ball up and out of the deep grass. You really need to hit it hard to get it out, and it will often fly a shorter distance than what you normally hit. The key adaptation needed here is to hit a club with a good deal of loft.[14] The loft of the club refers to the angle of the clubface and the degree to which it is vertical or angled back. A putter, for instance, has the lowest loft and is more vertical because you want the ball to roll on the ground toward the hole when you putt it rather than go up in the air on its way to the hole. Alternatively, wedges have the highest loft, and the clubfaces are more angled because they are used to hit the ball high and have the ball stop quickly on the green. A typical loft for a putter is 4 degrees, whereas wedges can have as much as 64 degrees of loft. To advance the ball in the long rough, use a more lofted club even if it means that you may need to adapt by hitting with a club that won't advance the ball the yardage required to get the ball onto the green. Hitting the more lofted club gives you a better chance of hitting the ball out of the rough and into the fairway where you can make an easier shot to the green while maintaining a good pace of play.

You will also have to adapt if your ball lands in the trees. Imagine your ball lying among a group of tall trees that stand between you and your target on the green. There can be small slivers of space between the trees that you might be tempted to try to hit your ball through with your shot. However, unless you have the accuracy of a professional golfer, you're likely to end up farther back than you currently stand if the ball misses the opening and hits the trunk of one of the trees in front of you. You could adapt by taking a club with a higher loft and

As a new golfer, I did everything possible to avoid the bunker. Hitting a shot out of the sand was not something I had confidence or skill to achieve. During a particularly important round where I was representing my organization at a corporate golf outing, I found myself in the bunker. I gave the difficult shot a try but didn't make it. Rather than melt into frustration trying to knock it out, I took the stroke penalty and went on with the round, saving myself and my playing partners a scene. Sometimes things don't go as planned and you are challenged to regroup and recover.

—Anna

trying to hit the ball over the trees, sacrificing distance for the chance to get out of the trees and advance the ball down the fairway. Alternatively, you could decide to hit sideways out of the trees rather than trying to advance the ball forward. This type of adaptation is referred to as "punching out" and is done with the intent of getting your ball out of the trees and into the fairway, leaving you with a good lie for the next shot. You can also choose to take relief from that spot if it is too challenging, but you will have to take a penalty shot.

Your ball might also land in a fairway bunker rather than the fairway. This too can require adaptations like what you might employ in the rough or trees. The ball may be buried in the sand. Like a ball in the deep rough, this shot will require you to use a club that is more lofted and hits the ball a shorter distance than what you might get from the club if you were in the fairway. You might also have to use a more lofted club if the ball is near the lip of the bunker. The lip of the bunker refers to the edge of the bunker walls. This section of a bunker can be very steep and make it difficult for you to advance the ball very far if the ball is very close to the lip.

You may also need to adapt from a networking perspective. We talked earlier about making small talk by asking questions of your special playing partner with escalating personal self-disclosure. The type of questions you ask and the rate at which you escalate from asking about the special playing partner to asking about them relative to others and you will depend on how they are responding to the questions. You may be able to escalate faster if the person is providing a lot of information about themselves and asking you questions in return. For instance, it's possible that your special playing partner may be a manager who brings up a position you're interested in applying for during your small talk in the fairway. If so, discuss the topic and don't worry so much about asking self-disclosure questions, because your special playing partner bringing up the promotion signals that they have progressed in the relationship to the point that they feel comfortable talking to you about business.

Alternatively, you may need to go slower in the rate at which you escalate the nature of self-disclosure questions if the person is not sharing a lot of information or not asking you questions that allow you to disclose things about yourself. This does not mean that the golfing experience is a failure. Rather, it means that more time may be needed to develop a relationship with the special playing partner. Go slow in this situation. The important point here is that there is no one-size-fits-all approach for using small talk in the fairway to build a relationship with your special playing partner. Each person is different, and you will need to adapt accordingly.

Empowerment

Choices surrounding adaptations in the fairway should be based on empowering you and your special playing partner. This requires you to adapt in ways that enable you and your special playing partner to play and network best. From a playing perspective, you are constantly faced with risk-versus-reward situations when deciding on what shot to hit from the rough, trees, or bunkers. The reward you can experience is hitting a great shot from a bad lie. However, the risk is that you may miss the shot, leaving you still in the woods or deep rough.

Playing in an empowering manner can mean that you don't try to hit the ball to the green if it's lying in a bad situation. Instead, a recovery shot that makes sure your poor tee shot does not cost you more than a stroke and allows you to maintain a good pace of play may be the best play.[15] Imagine you slice your drive and it ends up in the deep rough next to the fairway. You have 125 yards left to the green. Also, there is a water hazard right in front of the green. You face two challenges in this situation. The first is trying to advance the ball from the deep rough. The second challenge is the need to fly the ball onto the green so that you miss the water hazard. You could play as you might from the fairway and try to hit the ball out of the deep rough and onto the green. The reward is that you can possibly make a great shot if you land on the green. The risk is that you fail to get the ball out of the rough and must try to hit out of the rough again, adding strokes to your score and slowing down the pace of play each time you do so. There also is the risk that you won't hit the ball cleanly because of the long, thick grass in the rough, which could cause the ball to land in the water hazard, costing you a penalty stroke and a ball. The more empowering play is to hit a recovery shot that removes you from the bad lie in the deep rough and leaves you with a good lie in the fairway and the possibility to hit the next shot onto the green.

It can be easy to experience disempowering emotions when having to decide how to play from bad lies. Disempowering emotions in golf include the embarrassment of hitting a bad shot in front of others, the fear of not being able to get out of a bad situation, and the frustration of not being able to play as well as you want. These emotions are natural responses to a bad situation, but it is also important to recognize that they limit your physical and mental ability to play the game and network well during the golfing experience. Fear, for instance, can impair your performance by focusing your attention on the potential risks and limiting the attention you give to carefully examining the situation and considering alternatives.[16] Disempowering emotions can also impair you physically by triggering unwanted physical states like an elevated heart rate or clenched hands when you experience anger.[17] In these situations, you will likely hit poor shots because you swing too fast or grip the club too tightly.

The impact of disempowering emotions can spill over and impact your networking ability. Developing the rapport needed for nurturing a relationship with your special playing partner requires the golfing experience be an enjoyable one that allows a personal connection to develop between the two of you.[18] Letting your anger guide your actions and cause you to throw clubs or curse can make for a very unpleasant golfing experience for your special playing partner. It can also cause your special playing partner to experience vicarious embarrassment, which is a negative emotion others experience when in the presence of someone misbehaving.[19] Thus, letting disempowering emotions guide your actions will negatively affect you and can cause your special playing partner to experience disempowering emotions. The result is a golfing experience that is not enjoyable, which can limit conversation between you and your special playing partner and prevent a relationship from developing between the two of you.

Mindfulness

Being mindful of your emotional state during a golfing experience is important. Equally important in the fairway is to be mindful of your pace of play. Your pace of play is determined by how long it takes you to make your way to the ball and how long it then takes you to hit the ball.[20] Once you hit your drive, you should promptly drive your golf cart or walk to your ball. You don't need to hurry. However, try to avoid standing around for an excessive amount of time before hitting your next shot. You should also be sure to watch your shot land after you hit it. This will help you quickly find your ball. Good golf etiquette is for everyone to watch each other's shots so that they can help in finding balls that don't end up in the fairway. Thus, don't be hesitant about asking your special playing partner to help you track a ball after you hit it. Lastly, look for the yardage markers in the fairway as you make your way to your ball. This will help you spend less time figuring out the yardage for your next shot.

Once you arrive at your shot, promptly calculate the yardage using the yardage markers or a range finder if you have one. Knowing how far you hit each of your clubs ahead of time will help with pace of play because it will make it easier for you to pick a club once you have the yardage for a shot. Thus, spending time on the range figuring out how far you hit with each club will help with pace of play. There will be times when the yardage may be in between two clubs. For example, the shot may require you to hit the ball 145 yards and you know that you hit your 7 iron 145 to 155 yards and your 8 iron 135 to 145 yards. Don't take too long trying to decide if you should try to hit an 8 iron hard to have it fly its full distance or hit a 7 iron softly to have it fly the necessary yardage. It is recommended that you hit the longer club when you're uncertain, and following this guidance will help you make decisions quicker in the moment.[21] With your chosen club in hand, you are ready to take aim, get into your stance, and hit the ball.

There are many reasons why being mindful of pace of play in the fairway is important. First, a round of golf will take four hours or more to play.[22] That's a lot of time. In fact, the National Golf Foundation identified the amount of time it takes to play a round of golf as one of the major barriers keeping people from playing the game.[23] You should be mindful that your special playing partner agreed to invest a considerable amount of their time in spending time with you, and you should respect that investment. Adding to that time investment with your slow play does not respect the time commitment of your special playing partner and will likely dissuade them from accepting invitations to spend time with you in the future.

Second, slow play by any player adds to the time it takes everyone in the group to play the round. The beauty of golf is that everyone in your group plays the same holes at the same time. While this provides many opportunities for personal interaction, it also means that the time any golfer in the group takes adds to the amount of time for the whole group. Most golfers have an expectation that it will take approximately four hours to play a round and consider it bad golf etiquette to add to the time it takes to play a round with slow play. Not following golf etiquette and playing at a slow pace can lead your special playing partner to question your social competence, judgment, and understanding of the game of golf.[24] Thus, it is important to maintain a good pace of play or risk having your special playing partner develop negative perceptions about you.

Third, pace of play is important because of recent rules the USGA instituted to address the time it should take to play a shot. According to the rule, you should play a shot in less than forty seconds once your shot is free of interferences and distractions.[25] Interferences can be man-made or natural. A man-made interference could be caused by a cart path or course signage. You get free relief from these obstacles if they interfere with striking the ball, taking your stance, or making a swing. You take relief by dropping the ball from knee high within two club lengths of the ball's original position and no closer to the hole. An example of a natural interference would be if the ball embedded into the ground because of the wetness of the soil. You follow the same procedure when taking relief from a natural interference. A distraction occurs if you prevent a player from focusing on their shot. Talking on the phone or moving around in the line of sight while a player is in their stance about to hit the ball are examples of distractions. You are allowed time to address any interference or distraction but should hit the ball within forty seconds once they are removed to make sure you comply with the rules of golf.

One way to manage the pace of play is by choosing the right tee markers to play for the round. Hitting from tees further back means you are playing a longer course than if you play the tees more forward in the tee box. A longer course generally means more swings. More swings require more time. A longer course also creates more opportunity for your ball to end up in a hazard, a bunker, the rough, or the woods. Hitting from each of these situations slows down your pace of play. Being mindful in your selection of a set of tee markers can minimize these possibilities and reduce the amount of time it takes you to play each of your shots and the entire round.

A final but important way you can manage your pace of play is to be mindful of your stroke count as you play and be willing to stop playing a hole and pick up your ball if your stroke count gets too high on a hole. This is especially important when you're just beginning to play the game and find it difficult to hit the ball well. It's true that the rules of golf do not allow you to move the ball once it is in play. However, the USGA recently adopted the "maximum score" rule that allows for situations where a maximum score a player can get for each hole governs play.[26] It's important as a beginner that you and your special playing partner enjoy the experience, and having you hit shot after shot on the same hole will not allow that to happen. Remember, your primary purpose is to network, and your score is secondary to that goal. You can also be confident that your special playing partner will understand and not mind if you pick up on a hole that you're playing poorly. Realistically speaking, all golfers have picked up at some point during their time golfing.

How and when should you go about picking up your ball on a hole? If you feel you might need to pick up during a round, the first thing to do is let your special playing partner and others in your group know that you're just learning the game and may need to pick up if you have a bad hole. This will make sure it's not a surprise if you do pick up and will have the bonus effect of signaling your understanding of golf etiquette and the importance of pace of play. Then, when you need to pick up, say something to the effect of, "That's it for me. I'm going to pick up and start again on the next hole." Make sure to stay engaged in what is happening once you pick up. You have removed yourself from play, but you still need to be present to help with finding balls, fairway yardage markers, and the like. You also can still network, which is the primary reason for the golfing experience.

When to pick up is a judgment call. There is no rule of etiquette for it. One popular approach is to follow a "double par" process, whereby you pick up when your score for a hole gets to twice the par for the hole.[27] That approach would have you pick up when you get a six on a par 3, an eight on a par 4, or a ten on a par 5, giving you a double par score for the hole. Whatever approach you pick, be mindful to pick one that gives you an opportunity to try to advance the ball to the green, because that is the only way outside of practice that you're going to improve. There are also no formal rules for place of play. If you are playing with a group of your friends, you may decide to move your ball out of an obstacle or play a second ball for pace of play purposes. Just be sure to let your friends know what you've done. Always be attentive to the situation. If you are in a tournament, the rule will be that you must finish out the hole regardless of score or delay.

It is possible that slow play may not be your fault but due to the actions of your special playing partner. The challenge here is to stay in the moment and not let their slow play distract you. If your special playing partner's slow play does not occur regularly during the round, then it's easier to not fixate on the occasional slow play. Do something that can positively keep you in the moment like counting the number of trees on the hole when your special playing partner takes an excessive amount of time to play a particular shot. On the other hand, you may need to act if your special playing partner is slow to play every shot. One thing you can do is suggest that you play "ready golf" rather than play based on the honor system, which instructs whoever is farther from the hole on the fairway to play first. Doing so will help the pace of play and can remind your special playing partner to be mindful of pace of play.

Integrity

Landing in a hazard located in the fairway or adjacent to it can slow down your pace of play, especially if you do not know the rules for playing from these locations. Knowing the rules for playing your ball in hazards can help you know which actions are required to put your ball back into play, minimizing any time you add to the round because of an errant shot. Imagine there are white out-of-bounds markers going down the perimeter of the hole all the way to the green, and your drive from the tee box on the hole sliced a great deal and landed beyond the out-of-bounds markers. You are not allowed to play the ball where it lies when it goes out of bounds. Instead, the rules of golf require that you replay your shot from where you hit, meaning that you must tee the ball up again on the tee box and hit your drive again. You also must take a one-stroke penalty. Your ball going out of bounds in this situation did not add much time to play, allowing you to maintain a good pace of play.

Now imagine that you're on the same tee box and your drive slices a great deal. This time, however, the ball landed in front of the out-of-bounds marker, and it's not clear if it rolled past them. You then ride down in the cart to hit the ball, assuming it did not end up out of bounds. Upon arrival, you find out that the ball is out of bounds and you need to rehit your drive from the tee box based on the rules of golf. This requires you to drive all the way back to the tee box, get a tee and ball from your bag, go through your swing routine, and rehit your drive. Now you need to drive to your rehit drive in the fairway, go through your preshot routine, and finally hit the shot. All of this takes a lot of time and will surely slow down the pace of play.

A better approach when your shot to the fairway lands close to out of bounds is to hit a provisional ball. The rules of golf allow you to hit a second ball from the same spot where you hit your first if you are not sure if the first ball went out of bounds. Hitting a provisional ball prevents you from having to take the time to drive back to the tee box after going down and discovering that your first ball is out of bounds. To hit a provision, you simply need to tell the people in your playing group that you're unsure if your shot went out of bounds and you're going to hit a provisional ball. You then rehit your shot and proceed to find your first ball and determine if it is beyond the out-of-bounds markers. If so, you take the one-stroke penalty and play the provisional ball. If your first ball is not out of bounds, then you play the first ball and pick up the provisional ball. Hitting a provisional saves a great deal of time in this situation and will be greatly appreciated by your special playing partner.

This example described hitting a provisional when you're driving from the tee box to the fairway. The process of hitting a provisional ball when you're unsure whether a shot went out of bounds is the same if the shot was hit from the fairway, rough, woods, or bunker rather than the tee box. The only difference is that the rules require you to rehit the same shot rather than rehitting from anywhere in the tee box, so you should place the ball as close as possible to where it laid when you hit your original shot.

The challenge could be that your ball ends up in a water hazard rather than out of bounds. The water hazards will be denoted by a yellow or red line or yellow or red stakes around the perimeter of a water hazard. You do not play a provisional ball in this case. In fact, you can try to play the ball out of the water hazard even if this requires you to enter the water. Hitting from the water can be a risky and tough shot! Be sure you have a stable lie where you can place your feet before lining up to hit the ball so you don't lose your balance during the swing and fall into the water. You must make sure, however, that your club does not touch the water before you make your swing, or you will suffer a penalty stroke. You should only try to hit your ball out of the water hazard if any part of the ball is showing above the waterline.[28] Also remember that a ball is only considered in the hazard if all of it lies beyond the hazard marker. It is not considered in the hazard if any part of the ball is not past the hazard marker, and you can play it as a regular shot.

Imagine your ball is beyond the hazard marker and is completely submerged. The specific rule you follow depends on whether your ball is in a regular or lateral hazard. A regular hazard is denoted by a red line or stakes around the perimeter of a water hazard. To play from a regular hazard, you must take a penalty stroke and drop the ball anywhere behind the point where the ball entered the water and no closer to the hole.

The rule to follow is slightly different if the ball lands in a lateral hazard denoted by a yellow line or markers around the perimeter of the hazard. Like a regular hazard, there is a one-stroke penalty for dropping from a lateral hazard. However, the drop is different. Dropping from a lateral hazard requires that you drop the ball within two club lengths of the entry point and no nearer to the golf hole than where the ball entered the hazard.

No golfer wants to be out of bounds or in a hazard. Also, no golfer wants to add time to the golfing experience with their errant shots. Knowing the rules for playing when your ball goes out of bounds or into a hazard will help you more effectively manage your next shot and help you maintain good pace of play, ensuring the golfing experience stays positive and effective for networking with your special playing partner. It's now time to make our way to the green and learn how to be a leader at the end of each golf hole.

Leadership at
the Green

The green is the defined area of the golf course located at the end of each golf hole where the 4.25 inch hole each player is trying to get their ball into is located. The golf hole has not always been this size. The size varied during the early years of golf from course to course. However, the R&A established the size to be 4.25 inches in 1891, and that's the size it has remained ever since. The story goes that the current size of the golf hole is not based on any science or reasoning. Rather, it is said to have been based on the size of the pipe that was used by members at Royal Musselburgh Golf Club in Scotland to create a hole-cutter to consistently cut out a golf hole.[1] The pipe used in the invention was 4.25 inches, and the R&A used it as the basis for standardizing the golf hole size in 1891.

Like the fairway, the green is a mown area of the golf course, but it is more closely mown than the fairway. The closely mown nature of the green allows a golfer to roll the ball across the surface of the green toward the golf hole. There are several ways the ball can end up in the hole. The most common is for the ball to be lying on the green and putted into the hole. However, the ball may land in the hole as the result of a shot from off the green. One special situation where the ball goes into the hole from a shot made when the ball is not on the green is a hole in one, which occurs when a golfer's tee shot on a par 3 goes into the hole. This shot is a rarity in golf but is a moment of great pride for golfers. For example, professional golfer Meg Mallon recorded the most hole in ones on the LPGA Tour during the eighteen-year period from 1992 to 2020 but was only able to accomplish the feat eight times in that time span.[2] Hole in ones are even rarer for amateurs, making its occurrence a memorable experience for a golfer and one that often comes up when a golfer talks about their golf highlights.

There are special rules and etiquette on the green. For instance, it is the one place you are allowed by the rules of golf to mark and pick up your ball between shots. Many norms also come into play on the green like where you should stand when others in your group are playing their shots on the green and where you should walk relative to the balls of other golfers in your group. Knowing how to mark your ball and the different norms guiding play on the green is important because it signals your knowledge of golf and respect for the other golfers in your playing group.

From a networking perspective, the green is where all the golfers in your group come back together after having gone to the different areas of the golf hole to play their shots from the fairway or areas adjacent to the fairway like the rough or woods. Thus, the green is a moment of community much like the tee box and should be treated that way. Unfortunately, this is not always how the green area has been treated by golfers. Until 1961, the PGA of America had a "Caucasian-only clause" in its bylaws that prevented non-whites from playing in PGA-sanctioned tournaments.[3] In 1952, Charlie Sifford became the first man of color to play in a PGA-sanctioned tournament after the Caucasian-only clause was removed by the PGA under legal pressure from the attorney general of California. However, prior to the pressure applied by the California attorney general, the PGA was also under pressure from noted Black celebrities like Joe Louis, the great heavyweight boxer and activist, to allow men of color to play in PGA-sanctioned tournaments. This led the PGA to allow men of color to play in 1952 if they received a sponsor's exception. Most professional golf tournaments are sponsored events, meaning that a company financially supports the event and enables it to occur by providing money to the event organizers to run the event. In exchange, the sponsor receives public recognition for their support.

The first use of a sponsor's exception was in 1952 at the PGA's tournament in Phoenix. Charlie Sifford, Bill Spiller, and Ted Rhodes were Black men who received a sponsor's exception that allowed them to play in the tournament. The tournament organizers chose to have the three men play together rather than assign them to groups with white golfers. The organizers also chose to send the men out very early in the morning to play as the first group of the day and before the other professional golfers arrived at the course. When the men reached the green on the first hole, they found that the hole on the green had been filled with feces.[4] It was a rude reminder that not everyone welcomed the Black men into the tournament. While not as disgusting as what happened at the Phoenix tournament, racism still exists in golf today, and the green is an area where it can appear. Tiger Woods, for example, has described how, during youth tournaments, when he was leaving the green and making his way to the next tee box, his fellow competitors would make racist comments toward him.[5]

Racism, sexism, and other forms of bias can come out at any point on the golf course. Several aspects of the green make it a place where racism may be more likely to occur. First, it is where the final score for a hole is determined when the ball goes into the golf hole. The score is often higher than what a player hoped for when teeing off to begin the hole, and the anxiety and frustration of unmet expectations may cause people to act negatively toward others. Second, the end of play is also a time when golfers can take their attention off golf and focus on other matters as they make their way toward the tee box on the next hole. If a person holds racist or possibly sexist views, when the person is not focusing on playing, these thoughts may become the focus of attention and come out.

It is important to recognize that the green will also provide great opportunities for you to network with your special playing partner. You will have the opportunity to help each other read the green, when you try to understand how the ball may break as it rolls to the hole. Small talk is also possible as you make your way from the green to the next hole. You will also be able to celebrate each other's success in getting a good score or support each other when the score is more than you or your special playing partner hoped for. Let's now turn to discussing how you can be a leader and effectively manage the challenges and opportunities the green will present you during your golfing experience.

Strategy

Once on the green, your goal is to putt the ball into the hole in as few putts as possible. However, accomplishing this goal with a single putt, referred to as "one-putting," is not always going to happen and is even unlikely in most cases. Male professional golfers on the PGA Tour take an average of 28.94 putts during a round of eighteen holes, while female professional golfers on the LPGA Tour take an average of 30.05 putts per round.[6] Thus, both male and female professional golfers take more than one putt per hole and just under two putts per hole on average.

Given the averages for the professionals, a realistic approach to take on the green is to try to two-putt every green. This approach means that you should try to get the ball into the hole with one putt but don't get frustrated if it does not happen. Instead, recognize that there will be few times when it is realistic for you to expect to one-putt. As an example, analysis of putting data suggests you have only a 17 percent chance of making an 18-foot putt in one stroke.[7] Thus, the better goal is to ensure that you get the ball close enough to the hole that you have an easy second putt that allows you to easily putt the ball into the hole. Trying to two-putt every green will help you keep your score low by avoiding the dreaded three-putt, when it takes you three strokes with the putter to putt the ball into the hole.

Most golfers hate three-putting a green. One reason for the disdain of three-putting is that it adds strokes to your score. Three-putting also adds to the pace of play and other players in the group can get frustrated if it occurs frequently. Another reason why golfers feel so strongly about not three-putting is it can ruin an opportunity to take advantage of a good shot made from the tee box or fairway to the green. Imagine you're playing a par 4 and you hit a nice drive into the fairway from the tee box and a nice shot from the fairway onto the green. The expectation is that you should be able to get the ball into the hole in two strokes and walk away with a par or maybe a birdie if you happen to make the putt in one stroke. By three-putting, the score becomes a bogey 5, and the opportunity for successfully parring the hole is lost. Avoiding three-putting can be difficult. In fact, data suggest you have a greater chance of three-putting than two-putting once your ball is 36 feet or further from the hole on the green.[8]

One way to minimize the occurrence of three-putting a green as your ball gets farther from the hole on the green is to lag putt. When you lag putt, your immediate goal is not to make the putt but instead to putt in a way that ensures your ball will end up within a close distance to the hole, leaving you with a short and easy second putt. A good ending distance for the first putt is to finish within 3 feet of the hole because this distance of putt is made 95 percent of the time on average.[9] You'll need to practice lag putting. A good way to practice is to set four tees in the ground around a hole in the practice putting green. Place one tee 3 feet behind the hole, another tee 3 feet in front of the hole, and the other two tees 3 feet from the hole on either side. Then, practice lag putting from various distances, trying to make the ball stop within the circle created by the tees. Doing so will help you avoid the dreaded three-putt on the green.

From a networking perspective, your goal should be to use the green as an opportunity to recognize your special playing partner's good play on a hole because this will allow you to highlight the positive moment and ensure it becomes part of the shared golfing experience. The recognition can be based on your special playing partner getting par or better on the hole. Par is desired but not often experienced by the amateur golfer, given that the average amateur male golfer shoots twenty-four strokes over par on average while the average female golfer shoots thirty-six strokes over par on average.[10] Thus, you should recognize each time your special playing partner gets a par or better on a hole. A casual comment like, "Great score" or "You played that hole well" is all that is needed to show your recognition of your special playing partner's good play for a hole.

The same is true for putts on the green. Making a one-putt on a green is difficult, especially when the ball is far away from the hole. You should recognize one-putts that are made by your special playing partner on putts that are a reasonable distance from the hole. Recognize one-putts that are 10 feet or farther by saying something like, "Great putt" or "Great one-putt" as your special playing partner is making their way to get the ball out of the hole after scoring the one-putt. Compliments like this will help build your special playing partner's favorable attitude toward you according to research showing that people are prone to like someone more when the person compliments them.[11] This effect occurs even if the person receiving the compliment knows that the person giving the compliment has an ulterior motive.[12]

Curiosity

A lot of playing and networking activities happen on the green, and you will need to use your curiosity to respond effectively. From a playing perspective, putting is a simple back-and-forth motion, but it requires three pieces of information before you will be able to putt effectively. The three types of information are the speed, direction, and distance required for the ball to go into the hole. Golfers use the term "reading the green" to describe the process of collecting this information.

The speed of the green describes how quickly or slowly the ball will roll on the green. Putting on a fast green is like putting on a hard tabletop surface. The ball just keeps rolling and rolling even if you only slightly strike the ball with the putter. Alternatively, a slow green will require a more forceful strike from the putter. Most courses will keep the greens rolling at the same speed for all holes on the course. Several factors determine the speed of the green. The grass may be longer, which can slow down the ball as it rolls, making the green slower. The type of grass used for the green can also impact green speed, and the green will be slower if it has recently been sanded as part of the maintenance process. It is important to recognize all these factors when deciding the speed of a putt.

The speed of a green is measured using an instrument called a stimpmeter. The measurement process involves allowing a golf ball to roll down a rectangularly shaped metal tray and onto the green. The speed of the green is determined based on how far the ball rolls once it leaves the tray and lands on the green. The farther the ball rolls, the faster the green is. A study by the USGA found that the average green speed is 6.5 feet of roll for an average-paced strike of the golf ball.[13] For comparison, the average green speed on the PGA Tour and LPGA Tour is 11 feet,[14] almost twice what you will find at most courses.

The speed of the green is important to know because it will impact how hard you must hit the ball to have it travel a desired distance. Imagine you have a 10-foot putt and the green is running fast. Only a slight strike of the ball with the putter will result in the ball traveling the desired 10 feet, but a hard strike will be necessary if the green is slower. Speed also impacts how much the ball breaks as it rolls. Very few greens are completely flat. Instead, they have curvature that causes the ball to curve to the left or right as it rolls toward the hole. A faster green will cause the ball to react more to the curvature of the green as it rolls relative to a slower green.[15] Thus, the speed of the green will impact both how hard you strike the ball with the putter and where you aim your putt. The best way to gauge the speed of the greens at a course is to hit some putts on the green in the practice area and see how far they travel. You don't need to know the actual speed, but a sense of whether it is fast or slow will help you know what to expect on the course. You can also watch the golfers in your group as they putt on the green. Being curious about how far the ball goes when they putt will provide you with valuable information that you can use to understand the speed of your putt.

The break of your putt is another important piece of information to collect on the green. Golfers use this term when they are describing which direction the ball will roll on the green. The break is determined by the curvature of the green. How much the ball rolls to the right or left will depend upon the steepness of the curvature over which the ball will travel as it rolls toward the hole. The steeper the curvature, the more the ball will break, which will determine your aim for the putt. One way you can gauge the break is imagining a straight line running from the ball to the hole. If the area of the green to the right of the imaginary line is higher than the area to the left, the ball will break to the left as it rolls to the hole. Vice versa, the ball will roll to the right if the area to the left of the imaginary line is higher than the area to the right. Like with speed, it is also good to be curious and watch how the putts of your special playing partner and others in your playing group break when they putt the ball because it will help you better understand how your putt will break.

It is also important to know the distance of your putts on the green. Unlike in the fairway, there are no distance markers on the green. Some golfers will pace off the distance by walking from the hole back to their ball. Other golfers use their experience to know if a putt is short, medium, or long. One reason why golfers are not very scientific about measuring distance on the green is that how you putt the ball for a certain distance will depend upon the speed and curvature of the green. A 10-foot putt on a slow green will require a stronger strike, for example, than a 10-foot putt on a fast green. Add in curvature to the same 10-foot putt, and the force of the strike changes. Thus, the best approach is to consider distance in combination with the speed and curvature of the green when putting the ball.

It is also good to use your curiosity on the green for networking purposes by asking your special playing partner for help in reading the green when you are unsure. Seeking the advice of your special playing partner on the green can have several benefits for your relationship with them. First, it signals that you value your special playing partner's opinion and, by association, your relationship with

One of the great things about golf is that you can play a hole several times, but it will never play the same because of the speed and curvature of the green. I grew up in a single-parent household with my mom and younger sister. When I was young, my mom would drop me off at a local golf course when she had to work and had no place for me to stay. The golf course was a public nine-hole course. Yes, most golf courses have eighteen holes, but there are also shorter versions that have only nine holes. The green fee to play was only ten dollars because it was a public course and only had nine holes. What made it even more affordable was that they offered free replays, which meant that I could play the nine holes as often as I wanted in a day without having to pay additional green fees. I would play twenty-seven, thirty-six, and even forty-five holes some days, depending on when my mom got off work and picked me up from the course. Yet, despite playing the same hole three, four, or even five times in a day, it was never boring because my ball would always land on a different part of the green and these different locations resulted in different distance, speed, and curvature for putting.

—Eric

them. Second, according to research, asking for advice can make you come across as more competent to your special playing partner.[16] Given the positive impact competence has on building trust, asking for advice can help you nurture a stronger relationship with your special playing partner.

There are a few caveats to asking your special playing partner for advice on the green if you want it to help from a networking perspective. You need to use the advice or at least give it serious consideration. Otherwise, your request comes across as disingenuous and will potentially harm the relationship.[17] You should also not seek advice on every putt. The impact of seeking advice on perceptions of your competence is more likely to occur when you seek advice related to a difficult putt.[18] Thus, don't ask for help on a short putt that you are likely to make without any assistance. Instead, ask for advice about the 30-foot putt on the fast green that curves significantly, making it hard to read. Doing so will help you putt better on the green and network better with your special playing partner.

Adaptability

It is inevitable that some of your shots to the green will not end up on the green. Even if you're a very good golfer, you can expect to land on the green less than two-thirds of the time with your shots from the fairway, based on data indicating that most golfers hit the green 68 percent in regulation, meaning their second shot on a par 4 and their third shot on a par 5.[19] The expectation is even lower when we consider data showing that golfers with a 25 to 30 handicap (meaning their score is 25 to 30 strokes over par for a round of golf on average) land their shots in regulation on the green only 10 percent of the time.[20] The point being made with the data is that you will often need to adapt around the green.

Playing-wise, adaptation at the green will most often require a chip or pitch shot. A chip shot is a shot that you play when you're close to the green and want the ball to fly low in the air, land on the green, and roll out toward the hole. A pitch shot is played when you're further away from the hole and want the ball to go higher in the air and stop shortly after landing on the green. A chip shot and pitch shot are most often played when there is a need to get the ball up in the air so that you can fly over areas like the rough or a bunker located around the green. These shots can be difficult to play because they require accounting for both how far the ball must go in the air and how far it must travel on the green once it lands.

A safer shot when you're close to the green is to putt the ball if possible. Often, the rough may not be high around the green, which provides you an opportunity to putt from off the green where there are no hazards or bunkers between your ball and the hole. Putting onto the green is often easier than chipping or pitching because with putting you only need to account for the roll of the ball, but when you chip and pitch the ball, you must account for the ball flying in the air and the roll of the ball once it lands on the green.

The extra shots that are often required when you miss the green and need to chip, pitch, or putt the ball onto the green will add strokes to your score, making it unlikely you will score par for the hole and achieve your scoring goal. There also is the possibility that your pitch or chip shot onto the green will not land on the green or land on the green but leave you with a very long putt that may result in the frustrating experience of three-putting. Alternatively, the chip or pitch may go into the hole, creating cause for celebration. The disappointment or celebration that will accompany the final score for a hole, combined with the possibility of frustration or celebration with your chip and pitch shots around the green and putts on the green, will make the green where you and your special playing partner are likely to experience the most extreme emotions on the course.

It is important that negative emotional experiences that happen on the green not detract from the golfing experience. You don't want to let your negative emotions get in your way of being a good host and networking, nor do you want your special playing partner's negative emotions to become a barrier to an enjoyable experience during the round. An effective way to manage your own emotions and influence those of your special playing partner is through humor. Humor helps in this situation because it can ease the tension and anxiety that often accompanies the frustration of not getting the score wanted for a hole or hitting a poor shot around the green. This will prevent the negative experience from hampering your performance on future shots.[21] The shared experience of laughter can also nurture a stronger relationship between you and your special playing partner by promoting more openness and honesty in the sharing of thoughts and feelings.[22]

Not all humor is effective at managing the negative emotional experiences that can emerge on and around the green. The humor should be positive and not negative for it to be effective. Positive humor is good-natured and brings people together, whereas negative humor is mean-spirited and divisive. Positive humor promotes feelings supportive of strong relationships like empathy and tolerance, whereas negative humor promotes more hostile emotions and thoughts that can damage a relationship.[23]

One approach to using positive humor to help you and your special playing partner adapt emotionally to bad shots and bad scores is to reappraise the situation by focusing on the imperfections of golf and golfers in a jovial manner. Imagine, for example, that your ball is buried or plugged in the wall of the sand trap next to the green and it flies over the green when you strike it. You could experience anger that your ball ended up buried in the sand trap and frustration that your shot out of the bunker flew over the green. These are natural emotions that many golfers would feel in this situation. However, they will make it difficult for you to play well on the next shot and create the positive experience needed for a successful golf experience between you and your special playing partner. Instead, bring positive humor into the situation by laughing at the unlikely odds that your ball would end up plugged in the sand trap and the imperfect nature of the lies golfers can experience on a golf course.

Another method for bringing positive humor into the golfing experience is to use humor when sympathizing with the experiences of your special playing partner. Staying with the situation where your golf ball is plugged in the sand, now imagine that your special playing partner had a similarly difficult lie earlier in the round. You could jovially recognize the absurdity of you both getting such difficult lies in the sand during the round. You could also do the same if your special playing partner were to have a difficult lie in the sand trap later in the round after your experience in the sand. This form of positive humor where you respond to shared negative experiences in a jovial manner is known as affiliative humor, and it has been shown to enhance social interactions.[24] Other approaches include sharing an amusing story of a past golf experience related to what is causing a current negative emotional experience, laughing at yourself when you don't play or score as well as you would like, and using your wit to make a non-threatening and nonhostile observation.[25] These are all ways to use positive humor that can enable you and your special playing partner to positively adapt to any frustration or disappointment associated with playing a difficult game like golf.

Empowerment

Being a leader on the green also requires you to be empowering by helping your special playing partner perform better on the green. One way to be empowering is to ensure that you do not walk in the putting line of your special playing partner (or anyone in your playing group for that matter). The putting line is the path on the ground that the ball will travel as it rolls toward the hole when putted. You will not know exactly what line your special playing partner will decide to use until they get over the ball and putt it. However, make sure that you don't step on any of their potential putting lines because your step can alter the putting surface and impact the roll of the ball as it goes over the area where you stepped. The best approach in this situation is to walk outside of your special playing partner's ball as it lies on the green, keeping the ball between you and the hole as you walk past it on the green.

You can also be empowering by respecting the sight line of your special playing partner. The sight line represents the field of vision that a golfer sees as they stand over their ball on the green, ready to hit it toward the hole. It is important to stay out of the sight line when your special playing partner is putting because this will ensure that your presence is not a distraction to them as they concentrate on putting the ball into the hole in the fewest strokes possible. The best way to ensure you are not in a golfer's sight line when they are putting is to stand such that you can see their back as they stand over the putt. This will position you behind them and out of their sight line. It is also important to stand quietly while you wait for your special playing partner to hit their putt so that your movements don't distract them from making the best putt possible.

Your ball lying on the green could also be a distraction. To avoid this, it is best to mark your ball on the green until it is your time to putt. Generally, the rules of golf do not allow you to move your ball once it is put into play. However, you are allowed to mark and pick up your ball once it is on the green. The ball marker can be anything small, but it needs to be heavy enough that it won't get moved by the wind. You can buy special ball markers, or you can use a coin or any similarly shaped and sized object. Mark your ball by first standing behind the ball, being careful to make sure you are not standing in the putting line of another golfer on the green. Then place the ball marker on the ground directly behind and as close as possible to your ball without touching it. Once the ball marker is in place, you can pick up your ball and clean it in preparation for hitting your putt. Marking the ball removes it from the green, preventing it from being a visual distraction to whomever is putting. To put the ball back down on the green, first place the ball back in its original spot in front of the ball marker. Next, remove the ball marker without moving the ball. The ball is now in play and ready to be putted.

There can be instances when your ball marker is in the putting line of another golfer like your special playing partner. It is always good etiquette, if you sense your ball marker might be in someone's putting line, to ask, "Do you need me to move my ball marker?" If so, there is a special way to move your ball marker. First, ask the golfer which direction they want your ball marker moved. Let's say they ask you to move it to the left of where the ball marker currently lies on the green. You would then stand behind the ball marker, facing the direction you are going to move the ball. Next, place your putter head on the ground beside the ball with the toe, or end of the putter, pointing in the direction you are going to move it. Without moving the putter, pick up your ball marker from its current position and place it just past the toe of your putter. This moves the ball marker out of the way in the requested direction. It is important that you remember to replace your ball marker in its original position before hitting your putt. Failure to do so will result in a one-stroke penalty. To replace the ball marker, simply follow the same procedure you used to move the ball marker in reverse.

You are also allowed, and encouraged, to remove debris that may be in your putting line. The golf course is outside and thus prone to debris like twigs falling onto the green from trees close to the green, leaves being blown onto the green by wind, or sand landing on the green because of shots played from the greenside bunkers. This debris can interfere with your putt, and you are allowed to remove it without incurring a penalty stroke. However, be sure to put any debris you take off the green in a place that does not interfere with other golfers in your group or those who come to the green after you. In this way, you are empowering yourself and other golfers on the green.

Mindfulness

Mindfulness and maintaining focus on what's happening in the present on and around the green is also important. It can be easy to replay a bad shot to the green that left you in the greenside bunker or in deep rough around the green. It can also be easy to get ahead of yourself and start thinking about the upcoming hole, especially if it is a demanding hole or one that you think you may be able to play well. However, it is important to stay focused on what is happening at the green and the opportunity to network with your special playing partner. Success comes from staying mindful at the green.

One area where mindfulness is required concerns pace of play. There is a lot of information to collect when preparing to putt. You need to know the distance, speed, and direction the putt will travel, as we covered when discussing curiosity on the green. You should not wait until it is your turn to putt before collecting this information. The way to be mindful in this situation is to actively collect this information while you are making your way to the green. This can be accomplished by studying the green, looking for curvature as you approach. By doing so, you will be mindful of the opportunity to prepare while others are playing their shots, allowing you to maintain a good pace of play by being ready to step in and make your putt.

You can also be mindful and collect the needed information while other players are hitting their putts. Rather than losing yourself thinking about a past shot or an upcoming shot, use this time to read the green by scanning for curvature that can cause the ball to curve as it rolls toward the hole. You can also be mindful by scanning for uphill and downhill slopes that can cause the speed of the putt to be slower or faster, respectively. Also, staying in the moment and watching the putts of other golfers can provide invaluable information related to speed, direction, and distance. The point is to be mindful of the opportunities available on and around the green to prepare yourself to putt and maintain a good pace of play.

Mindfulness is also important when you're not on the green and must hit a chip or pitch shot. Imagine your shot from the fairway came up 10 yards short of the green, leaving you with a short pitch shot onto the green. You arrive at the green in your golf cart, take your pitching wedge out of your bag, and walk over to hit the pitch shot onto the green. After hitting the shot, you then go back to the golf cart, put the pitching wedge in your bag, and take out your putter before heading to the green to putt. The problem here is that you are not playing in a manner that is mindful of pace of play. It would be better to take both your pitching wedge and your putter with you when you go to hit the pitch shot. Then, you can proceed directly onto the green to putt after hitting the pitch shot, rather than returning to the cart, switching your pitching wedge for your putter, and then having to walk back to the green to putt. Having both clubs with you is being mindful of how you are impacting pace of play and will be much appreciated by your special playing partner.

You should also be mindful of your impact on course conditions on and around the green. The green is a closely mown area, and this condition leaves it vulnerable to a divot, representing a cut or indentation in the green caused by the landing of a golf ball. A divot can easily occur when you hit a shot from the fairway that lands hard on the green because of the speed or height of the shot. It can be easy when celebrating a shot that landed on the green from the fairway to forget to check if it left a divot where it landed. Usually, the divot is some distance away from where your ball finally settles, so it may not interfere with your putt. However, not being mindful to check for a divot can impact the play of golfers who come after you to play the hole and can send a signal to your special playing partner that you're not concerned about being accountable for the impact you are having on the course and potentially other golfers.

Repairing a divot requires a tool. You can buy special divot repair tools, and we recommend you have one as part of the accessories you carry during the round. The divot repair tool usually has two or three prongs on the end and a small handle to grip it. Repair the divot by inserting the prongs into the ground just outside of the divot and pushing the ground up and toward the divot. Repeat this process all around the perimeter of the divot and then pat down the ground with your putter to make a smooth surface on the green.[26] You can also use a tee and follow the same repair process if you happen not to have a divot repair tool with you.

Your play can also affect the condition of the bunkers, and you should be mindful to repair your impact. Hitting out of a bunker requires that you hit into the sand behind the ball to create an explosive shot of sand that will carry the ball out of the bunker. This will cause the sand in the bunker to become uneven. You should be mindful to repair the impact of your shot by using the rakes provided at each bunker to rake the sand and leave the area you hit out of as smooth as possible for the next golfer who is unlucky enough to land in the same bunker. Sand from your shot out of the bunker may also land on the green. The sand may not interfere with your putt, but a mindful approach to playing on the green is to sweep this sand off the green with your hand or a towel. This action will send a signal to your special playing partner about your mindfulness and your respect for other golfers.

Integrity

The order in which golfers on the green putt depends on their respective distance from the hole, and it is important to respect this order of play. In fact, the rules of golf allow a player to be assessed a penalty stroke for putting out of order on the green. It doesn't happen often in noncompetitive rounds, but a player can ask you to rehit your putt and take a penalty stroke if you hit out of order. To understand the order of putting, imagine you, your special playing partner, and two other golfers in your foursome are on the green and you happen to be farthest from the hole and your special playing partner is the next farthest. You have the honor of putting first because you are farthest from the hole. Your special partner would then putt next if your putt ended up closer to the hole than their ball. However, you would hit your second putt if the ball remained farther from the hole after your first putt stopped. You might hear someone in the group say, "You're still out" to recognize that you still have the dubious honor of putting before anyone else in the group. This situation occurs most often when everyone's ball is close to the hole and you happen to hit the ball too softly or too hard.

There are a few exceptions to this rule. In the scenario just discussed, your special playing partner's ball is the second farthest from the hole, and you could ask them to putt if you are not ready to putt. For example, you may have left your ball marker in the golf cart and could ask your special playing partner to putt while you go back and get the ball marker rather than slowing up play while you retrieve it. Another situation where you may not follow the distance rule in determining the order of putting is when you want to "finish" putting. The rules of golf allow you to putt continuously on your turn until you putt the ball into the hole.[27] This means that you could hit your second putt immediately after your first putt if the first putt did not go into the hole. The continuous rule would also allow you to hit your third putt immediately if the second putt missed and so forth.

While continuous putting is allowed, most golfers only putt this way if the putt they just hit ends up very close and can be easily putted into the hole. This is done to speed up play. It is generally frowned upon to follow continuous putting if you require time to prepare for hitting your next putt. In the previous scenario, it would be good for pace of play for you to walk up and putt your ball into the hole if it ended up only a few inches from the hole after your original putt. However, it would not be advisable for you to hit your next putt if the putt ended up several feet from the hole and you needed to collect information on speed, direction, and distance before putting it again. Doing so would slow down play and not be respectful of the other golfers in your group.

The role of distance in determining order of play also applies if one or more of the golf balls in the group are on the green and one or more golf balls are off the green. For example, your ball and those of the other two golfers in the group may be on the green and a good distance to the hole while your special playing partner's ball is just off the green but closer to the hole. Whoever's ball is farthest from the hole plays first, regardless of whether it is a golfer on the green like yourself in this situation or a golfer off the green like your special playing partner.

The rules of golf are constantly changing, and there are two recent rule changes related to the green that you should know. The first rule change concerns the flag and whether you can putt with the flag in the hole. Until recently, the rules of golf assessed a penalty stroke if a player putted the ball on the green and it struck the pin in the hole. For this reason, the pin was always taken out of the hole before anyone putted. This rule has since been changed, and you can putt with the pin in the hole without incurring any penalty. There has been a great deal of debate among golfers about whether you should putt with the flag in the hole or out of the hole. The evidence is mixed, but some research suggests you have a slightly better chance of making a putt if the flag is out of the hole.[28] Since the difference is not large, the best way to decide is to consider pace of play because it can add time to take the flag out and then replace it. Thus, leave the flag in if your group is playing slow. You should also check with your group prior to pulling the flag from the hole. There may be somebody in the group who wants the flag in when putting. Also, you may get asked to "tend" the flag, which means to hold the flag in the hole while the other person is preparing and putting. The respectful thing is to ask if they would like the flag to be left in or pulled.

The second recent rule change relates to the ball moving while on the green. Previously, a golfer was assessed a penalty stroke if their ball moved while they were standing ready to hit their putt and they had to replace the ball in its original position. The penalty stroke was applied regardless of whether the golfer caused the ball to move or some other factor like the wind caused it to move. Fortunately, the USGA and R&A recently changed this rule, and a golfer is now only assessed a penalty if they cause the ball to move while preparing to putt it.[29] You still must replace the ball in its original position if it moves, but you no longer are assessed a penalty if it moves for some reason other than your actions.

Lastly, integrity in following the rules of golf also comes into play with recording your score. Each hole ends at a green, so this is where your final score for each hole is determined. You can keep your own score, but often someone will keep the score for the entire group using a scorecard provided by the course. Thus, players commonly share their score with the person keeping the group scorecard after each hole. This generally does not create any awkward situations, but there is the possibility that it can if someone in the group reports a score for a hole that doesn't seem correct based on their play for the hole. Reporting your score accurately is a must if you want to act with integrity on the golf course, so any doubtful reporting raises concerns about someone's honesty.

You will have to manage this awkwardness if you are the one keeping score for the group. Do you simply write down what someone in the group reports if you know for a fact that they should be reporting a different score? What if the person just forgot about a stroke by mistake and with no malintent? This is easy to do on a par 5 when you are hitting several shots. Do you confront them about their score? What if the reason for the misreporting is that the person doesn't think they deserve to take a penalty stroke because they got an unlucky break when their ball hit off a tree and went into a water hazard. Do you simply write down what they report to you on the scorecard? The truth is you don't know why the person misreported the score. Rather than challenging their integrity, the better approach is to act with integrity yourself and provide them with an opportunity to correctly report their score. For example, you could suggest what you thought they got as a possibility by saying something like, "I thought you had a bogey on that hole" when they reported a par for the hole and you know for certain their score should be a bogey. Acting in this way provides the person with an opportunity to reconsider their score or reveal to you the accuracy of their reported score without you directly challenging their integrity. You can also use this situation to gain a better understanding of your special playing partner when they report their score. A simple mistake of miscounting or accidentally forgetting a stroke usually occurs once in a round and is to be forgotten. However, a special playing partner who regularly misreports their score on the golf course can also be expected to act without integrity off the golf course, and you should keep this in mind when you interact with this person in the future.

There are a great many opportunities for leadership both on and around the green. Demonstrating your leadership at these times will contribute to a positive golfing experience and successful networking with your special playing partner. The last green during the round is especially important because it is where you will make your invitation to have your special playing partner join you at the nineteenth hole, otherwise known as the clubhouse, for socializing and potentially talking business. Let's now turn to talking about leadership at the nineteenth hole.

Leadership at the Nineteenth Hole

"The nineteenth hole" is a special term used to describe the food and beverage area of the clubhouse where golfers often congregate to socialize after a round of golf. The first recorded use of the term was 1890 in a Scottish newspaper called *The Evening Telegraph* where the nineteenth hole was used to describe the place golfers would meet for supper after a round of golf.[1] The number nineteen is used in the term to signify the place to meet after the eighteen holes of a round have been played by golfers who want to celebrate their good play or drown their sorrows if they hit too many bad shots.

The nineteenth hole is also where you can stop focusing on playing golf and give more attention to socializing and networking with your special playing partner. Hopefully, you've spent the time during the round using golf to create positive shared experiences with your special playing partner. The nineteenth hole is where you can use those experiences and knowledge gained through small talk during the round to further nurture the relationship with your special playing partner. Importantly, it is considered appropriate to have more business- or career-related discussions at the nineteenth hole. These types of conversations can occur during the round, especially if your special playing partner brings them up during your small talk on the course, but in case they haven't been discussed, the nineteenth hole is where you can bring them into the conversation with your special playing partner.

Golfers aren't required to spend time at the nineteenth hole. Thus, it is important to be prepared to invite your special playing partner to join you after the round for food and beverages in the clubhouse. However, you also need to be prepared for your special playing partner to not join you in the nineteenth hole for some personal or professional reason. Yet making the invite is not when being a leader at the nineteenth hole begins. It begins when you first arrive at the course and have an opportunity to visit the food and beverage area and identify certain tables or spots that will be most conducive to socializing and talking business with your special playing partner.

The nineteenth hole also presents challenges in addition to the opportunities it provides for networking with your special playing partner. Introducing beverages into the golfing experience means that being a leader at the nineteenth hole also requires managing yourself if you decide to drink alcohol when socializing. The potential for alcohol consumption also requires being prepared for awkward or inappropriate situations with your special playing partner or others in the group.

It is also important to remember that the nineteenth hole has not always been open or welcoming to everyone. Private golf clubs have denied access to women, people of color, or both throughout the history of golf in the United States, and it continues today. It is not illegal to bar women from joining if the golf club is a private club. In fact, the ability to do so has been upheld by the US Supreme Court, which ruled that the first amendment of the US Constitution protects the ability of private clubs to restrict membership based on gender.[2]

Fortunately, there are only a handful of private clubs left in the United States that do so, and even clubs that held out for a long time are now changing. Augusta National Golf Club, site of the major men's golf tournament known as The Masters, only opened its membership to Black men in 1990 and to women in 2012. While access to golf and the nineteenth hole for women and people of color is increasing, there are still instances where a group is not made to feel completely welcome. Burning Tree Club, for example, is a private and exclusive golf course in Bethesda, Maryland, that recently started accepting women as members but as of this writing does not provide locker rooms or bathrooms for women.[3]

Thus, the uncertainty of whether your special playing partner will accept your invitation to the nineteenth hole, the introduction of alcohol into the experience, and the potential discriminatory or disrespectful practices of others each contribute to making the nineteenth hole a challenging spot for networking. At the same time, it also presents a unique opportunity. The broader topics that can be discussed and the longer time that can be given to talking about them at the nineteenth hole present unparalleled opportunities for you to develop a richer relationship with your special playing partner. Capitalizing on this opportunity while navigating the potential challenges requires leadership at the nineteenth hole. Let's talk about how you can be a leader at the nineteenth hole.

Strategy

The main goal at the nineteenth hole is to take the relationship with your special playing partner to a higher level of engagement. During the round, your

In 2007, Tiger Woods and the PGA Tour announced that the AT&T National would be held at Congressional Country Club in Maryland. At the time, I was a vice president at the Congressional Hispanic Caucus Foundation, directing a leadership development program for Latinx interns from all over the country. I was also hooked on golf. In a crazy stroke of luck, I was invited to play Congressional on the day before the tournament began alongside journalists, philanthropists, and other nonprofit partners. It was even rumored that we would meet Tiger Woods at the nineteenth hole.

I arrived at the course bright and early, in a state of high excitement. Congressional Country Club is a spectacular, pristine golf course, and it was in top form for the coming tournament. Prior to Congressional, I had only played on municipal courses that often did not receive the same level of maintenance as a country club like Congressional. I knew this was going to be an experience to remember.

The first thing I noticed was that the line of men waiting to take my clubs to a cart were almost all Black. It was noteworthy, but I decided to shrug it off. I was assigned a caddy from this group, and off we went. The next thing I noticed was that I was one of very few women on the course and probably the only woman of color. My caddy was incredibly supportive, encouraging me and setting me up for success along the way. We both rejoiced when I parred a hole. He confided in me that many people thought women couldn't play Congressional. We set out to prove them wrong.

Out on the course I noticed that the landscape maintenance crews were predominately Latino men. It was starting to feel uncomfortable. I wrapped up the round, hugging and tipping my caddy, who had really helped me enjoy the experience. I entered the clubhouse with the three other men in my foursome wondering what to expect. There was a reception inside where everyone was waiting for Tiger Woods to arrive. The guests were almost entirely white men. I was one of a handful of women in the room. The promise of meeting Tiger Woods and my fierce curiosity kept me riveted to my spot. We eventually did hear from Tiger, but I left the event with a sense of unease. Under different circumstances, I might not have lingered to relax at the nineteenth hole.

—Anna

engagement consisted of playing golf together and participating in small talk in between shots. This engagement provided you and your special playing partner with the opportunity to get through the early stage of relationship development whereby you learned about each other and gained a sense of each other's commonalities and differences.[4] Playing-wise, you learned about the other's strengths and weaknesses on the course. You also saw how each other responded to adversity and success. The time during the round also provided you each an opportunity to share information about your respective lives at a personal level. This type of information is typical of early-stage relationship development.

Now, at the nineteenth hole, you can move the relationship to a higher level where you move from small talk to actual conversations that involve sharing more varied and intimate information between you and your special playing partner. On the course, the focus is golf, and most of your questions and small talk should be about golf, along with some nonintrusive questions that allow for self-disclosure by your special playing partner. The topic can change at the nineteenth hole, where the focus is less golf and more business. At this point, it is acceptable and appropriate to ask more professional questions related to why you initially invited your special playing partner to join you for a round of golf. It is appropriate because you were intentional when you invited the person and let them know that you wanted to talk about a specific professional topic in addition to playing a round of golf with them. It is also appropriate because the topic you want to discuss likely requires an in-depth discussion rather than small talk between you and your special playing partner. You can now have a more in-depth conversation at the nineteenth hole because you don't have to focus on playing golf, allowing you both to give your undivided attention to the topic you wanted to discuss.

You also can ask more intimate questions of your special playing partner to learn more about them and advance the relationship. Asking intimate questions may feel awkward, and you may fear that you will come off as prying. One way to nurture intimacy is to offer it yourself. For instance, you can share your long-term professional goals with your special playing partner if the person happens to be a leader in your organization who can help you move toward achieving your long-term goals. Alternatively, you could share your frustrations at not being able to get an appointment with someone at your special playing partner's organization if the special playing partner is a leader at a company you seek as a customer. You can motivate your special playing partner toward sharing more intimate information by doing so first.[5]

Intimacy between you and your special playing partner is also possible through supportive interactions. There will undoubtedly be some poor shots and bad holes scoring-wise during the round. Empathizing with your special playing partner in these moments can help promote greater intimacy between you and them.[6] Imagine that your special playing partner had a great round going until the last two holes when they scored bogey-bogey to just miss breaking 80 with their score and are noticeably upset about the end of the round. You can empathize with their disappointment by saying, "Those last two holes were tough. But overall, you played a great round and should be proud of the way you played today." Recognizing that the last two holes were difficult allows you to show that you understand the challenge your special playing partner faced when playing them. Then, by focusing on the whole round, you offer your special playing partner an alternative perspective to consider that can help them better manage their negative experience. Using this pattern of offering recognition followed by an alternative perspective is the key to being both genuine and effective when showing empathy.[7]

Advancing the relationship with your special playing partner should culminate in setting the stage for the two of you to socialize online or offline after the golfing experience has ended. A simple way to support this is to ask your special playing partner to connect with you on a professional social media site like LinkedIn. You will need to have a professional-looking LinkedIn profile set up before you ask your special playing partner to connect with you. At this point, we wouldn't recommend asking the person to connect with you on more personal social media sites like Facebook or Instagram unless you feel comfortable with the person being able to know about your personal life. Keeping the connection to professional social media sites can also minimize awkward situations whereby your special playing partner interprets that your interest in them is personal and not professional. You can avoid this situation by only asking them to connect with you on professional social media sites.

You should also seek face-to-face engagement with your special playing partner after the round through another round of golf, meeting for coffee, or another form of in-person engagement. Your special playing partner's responses to these requests will tell you a lot about how they experienced the golf outing and how they perceive their relationship with you. A "yes" indicates they had a positive experience and positively view their relationship with you. If so, congratulate yourself on a successful use of golf for networking and accessing leadership. A "no" doesn't necessarily mean that your special playing partner had a negative experience, but it does mean that the relationship is still in the formative stages and will need further nurturing. In that case, achieving your networking goal may require a more long-term approach involving multiple instances of engagement where you can create the shared experiences and information sharing required for developing a strong professional relationship.

Curiosity

Using the nineteenth hole for relationship development will require curiosity in the form of asking questions of your special playing partner when you socialize after the round. The first question is the invitation asking your special playing partner to join you in the clubhouse. You can make the invitation at any time during the round, but the most common time is when you're later in the round. For example, you can ask your special playing partner to join you at the nineteenth hole around the fifteenth or sixteenth hole. This way, if they say yes, you know you are walking off the eighteenth green together to the clubhouse. You can also make the invite at the eighteenth hole. The round will finish on the eighteenth green, and it is customary for all golfers in a group to shake hands and thank each other for playing the round. This occurs after the last person has made their final putt while everyone is still on the green and is done quickly to avoid holding up the next playing group hitting to the eighteenth green.

Regardless of when you make the invitation, you will want to tap into the positive experience of the round by saying something like, "Thanks for accepting the invitation to join me today. Let's finish up the outing over some food or a beverage before you leave. What do you say?" This form of invite accomplishes several things. First, it thanks your special playing partner for joining you, expressing your gratitude in the process. Showing gratitude is important because it signals the value you place on the relationship and can motivate mutually responsive behavior on the part of your special playing partner like accepting your invite to the nineteenth hole.[8] Second, the invite focuses on the nineteenth hole as a continuation of the round of golf rather than a separate event and decision to be made by your special playing partner. This aspect of the invite is important because it leverages the influence of consistency on how people respond to requests. Research has shown that people like to act in a consistent manner and respond to requests that allow them to do so.[9] The example invite reminds your special playing partner that they accepted your invitation to join you for a round of golf. Responding to your request now to join you at the nineteenth hole would be consistent with the acceptance of your original request and thus is more likely to be accepted than a situation where your special playing partner does not see an acceptance as consistent with their prior behavior.

Once the request is accepted, you can then make your way to the nineteenth hole with your special playing partner and ask questions about a host of topics. At a personal level, you'll want to discover their preferences related to food and beverages by asking, "What can I get for you?" when you enter the clubhouse. Always ask your special playing partner for their food and beverage requests first so you can follow their lead in choosing whether to order alcohol. At a social level, you should ask questions about the round like, "What did you hit to the green on the ninth hole?" if the person hit a well shot in that instance. Topics like these give you an opportunity to socialize with your special playing partner and develop the relationship in the process.

Most importantly, make sure you ask questions related to the professional reason that motivated you to ask the special playing partner to the golf outing. If you're interested in learning about an opening in your company, you can ask about the opening in an open-ended manner. Imagine you work in the finance department and are interested in a managerial opening. You invited the vice president of finance from your company to play a round of golf with you and let them know when you made the invite you wanted to use the time at the golf course to learn more about opportunities in your firm for advancement. Now is the time to ask something like, "I hear they're looking for a manager in finance. Do you know what kind of person they're looking to put in the position?" and obtain answers to your questions about career advancement opportunities in your firm.

Your interest in making the original invite might involve someone external to your firm. Maybe the person you invited is an officer who works at a company you hope to acquire as a new customer. When you made the invitation, you indicated to them that you hoped to learn more about their business during the round so you could identify ways your company could help their company as a supplier. Now is the time to follow through on your invite and ask a question like, "So what are the things about your business you're most challenged by at the moment?" or you might say, "I'd like to learn more about the production challenge you mentioned when we were playing" if your special playing partner shared at some point in the round that production at their company is a challenge.

Lastly, you'll want to use your curiosity to help you accomplish the objective of engaging with your special playing partner after the round. A question like, "Are you on LinkedIn? I'd like to connect with you if you are" supports engagement after the round on social media. Additionally, you'll want to set up a follow-up, in-person meeting to continue the conversation about the focal professional topic that motivated your invite. A simple request like, "So glad you were able to join me today. It was a lot of fun. I would like to follow up on our conversation today. Do you have any time next week for a coffee when we could talk more?" would be the type of invite that can create the opportunity for a follow-up meeting that will enable the relationship to continue to develop and allow you to pursue your professional career aspirations.

Empowerment

Empowering yourself and your special playing partner to socialize and converse with each other at the nineteenth hole requires you to create a context or environment conducive to conversation. To do this, it's beneficial to survey the layout of the food and beverage area before your round starts. You can walk over and examine the area after checking in for your tee time at the pro shop when you arrive at the course. The food and beverage area in the clubhouse will have small tables and chairs. It will often also have a large television that is likely tuned to a live golf broadcast or some other sporting event. It's good to identify a spot that is most conducive to spending time with your special playing partner after the round. You will want to account for noise and distractions that can interfere with your conversation with your special playing partner. Therefore, pick a table within view of the television but far enough away that you and your special playing partner will be able to easily hear each other. Sitting too close to the television can cause you to raise your voice, and you probably don't want everyone in the room to hear the conversation between you and your special playing partner. A table toward the back of the room usually works well and is more likely to be open when your round ends because it is farther away from the television.

You should also be sensitive to seating order because it can influence your ability to have a conversation. You will want to sit beside your special playing partner, as a conversation is more likely to occur between individuals when they can easily interact with each other.[10] Sitting across the table from your special playing partner will make it more difficult to interact. No one likes to be told what to do, so don't be too direct and say something like, "You sit here" when establishing the seating order. A more effective way is to use a prop. For example, most golfers wear a hat to protect themselves from the sun. If you are wearing a hat, you can establish who sits where using your hat to reserve a chair and asking your special playing partner to join you in an adjacent chair. A casual statement like, "Let's leave our hats in these seats while we wash up in the locker room" should be sufficient to ensure that you can sit close enough to have a conversation with your special playing partner at the nineteenth hole.

In addition to creating the right environment, you also need to empower your special playing partner to join you in a conversation. One way to accomplish this is to ensure that you don't dominate the conversation. Instead, support conversation with your special playing partner by introducing topics. The experiences from the golf outing provide a good initial focus, but you will want to eventually move the focus of the conversation to your professional reason for inviting the special playing partner to join you for a round of golf.

Integrity

Integrity is also important at the nineteenth hole. Time spent socializing often includes eating and drinking because you've just played eighteen holes and are hungry and thirsty from the experience. Alcohol is often available at the nineteenth hole, and managing this aspect of the experience requires integrity on your part. You will want to respect your special playing partner's preference when it comes to including alcohol in the experience at the nineteenth hole. You should not try to pressure your special playing partner to drink if they indicate they do not want an alcoholic drink when you ask them what food and beverage they would like. They may not want to drink for any number of reasons, and you should respect their decision not to drink without asking why. Even further, you should follow the preference of your special playing partner if they don't drink alcohol and not drink alcohol yourself.

Following the lead of your special playing partner when it comes to drinking alcohol is recommended for several reasons. First, it prevents alcohol from being a point of difference between the two of you. Commonalities between you and your special playing partner serve as the basis for developing a relationship. Drinking alcohol when your special playing partner isn't drinking highlights a difference between you and them that may not be beneficial to the relationship. Second, alcohol impairs your ability to think and could cause you to say or do something that you regret. The same amount of alcohol that you are used to drinking can be too much when you've just finished playing eighteen holes of golf over several hours out in the hot sun. It is easy to get dehydrated in this situation, and drinking alcohol when you are dehydrated causes the impact of the alcohol to be greater, making it more likely that you will become inebriated and potentially do or say something you regret. Your special playing partner is likely to notice and frown on any misbehavior caused by your alcohol consumption.

Given that 86 percent of adults in the United States report they have drunk alcohol at some point in their lifetime, it is likely that your special playing partner may choose to drink alcohol at the nineteenth hole. Caution is required if your special playing partner and you do decide to add alcohol to your socializing. Sharing a beer or drink can be a bonding experience. However, you want the shared experience to be a positive one. A good way to accomplish this is by drinking moderately and not overindulging to the point that you say or do something inappropriate or act illegally by driving home while inebriated. You should also take note of the amount drunk by your special playing partner and offer to drive them home or pay for a taxi if you believe they are unable to drive safely.

You can decide not to drink alcohol regardless of your special playing partner's preferences. For example, research has shown that alcohol consumption can increase the likelihood of sexual assault because of its psychological effects.[11] Thus, if you are a woman, you may feel safer not drinking. Alternatively, you simply may not like the taste of alcohol or you may not believe it is appropriate to drink alcohol when you're with a fellow employee, potential client, or any similar type of professional associate. You are not alone in this belief. According to a survey of five hundred HR professionals, 60 percent felt it inappropriate to drink alcohol when spending time with a client and 78 percent felt it inappropriate when having a meal with a coworker.[12] The reason why you choose not to drink does not matter. What matters is that you respect your choice and not drink alcohol.

A challenge if you decide not to drink but your special playing partner does is how to prevent the difference in drinking preferences from being a barrier to networking. One recommendation is to order club soda with ice and a lime in a highball glass and wrap a napkin around the glass. This approach capitalizes on research showing that people have norms or expectations about what should be drunk in different types of containers.[13] The highball glass is typically associated with alcoholic drinks, so most people will believe that your drink is alcoholic since it is being served in a glass often used to consume alcohol. Putting a clear beverage like club soda in the glass makes it uncertain to an observer whether you are drinking water or a clear alcohol like vodka or gin. Ice and lime are often accompaniments to a vodka or gin drink, so adding them can lead an observer to infer that the clear liquid is an alcohol. Lastly, wrapping a napkin around the glass helps to limit what the other person sees to just the lime and ice, which are common accompaniments to alcoholic drink. Your special playing partner will likely know that you are not drinking alcohol or may even ask you what you're drinking. The point is not to lie or mislead them. However, the recommended club soda and highball approach allows you to look like you are sharing a drink with your special playing partner while being respectful of your choice not to drink.

Mindfulness

The nineteenth hole is also where you need to be mindful of the type of round you and your special playing partner just finished. You can start socializing and not be concerned with other things happening at the clubhouse if the event was a "buddy" round involving you and your special playing partner. However, the situation changes if you just played in a charity event or company outing. If this is the case, you and your special playing partner are part of a larger group event, and you should be mindful of the activities going on with the event. For instance, there may be raffle announcements, auctioneering, and presentations by individuals from the nonprofit or cause benefitting from the charity event. Similarly, company-sponsored outings may include recognition of employees, company announcements, and comments provided by leadership. You should be mindful of these activities and incorporate them into your socializing by giving your attention to them when they are occurring and bringing them into the conversation with your special playing partner when appropriate and beneficial to your socializing.

You also should be mindful to settle any golf bets between you and your special playing partner. You can choose ahead of time whether to include betting in the golfing experience. The two most common types of betting are Skins and Nassau bets. In Skins bets, the player with the best score on a hole wins a designated amount for the hole. If the golfers involved in the Skins bet tie on a hole, the winnings for that hole are pushed to the next hole. Imagine you and your special playing partner agree to play a Skins bet for the round and designate $1.00 to be won on each hole. You then tie on hole 1. The $1.00 from hole 1 is then added to the $1.00 for hole 2, meaning that the Skins bet is worth $2.00 on hole 2. Whoever wins hole 2 by having the lowest score wins $2.00, composed of the $1.00 pushed from hole 1 and the $1.00 designated for hole 2. If you both tie on hole 2, then the bet from hole 1 ($1.00) and the bet from hole 2 ($1.00) get pushed to hole 3, which would then be worth $3.00 to whomever has the best score on the hole.

A Nassau bet counts how many holes are won by each golfer, and the golfer with the best score on the most holes is the winner. There are usually three bets with a Nassau that designate an amount to win for the most holes won on the front nine, most holes won on the back nine, and most holes won for the eighteen holes in total. For example, imagine you and your special playing partner have agreed to a $5.00 Nassau bet. You have the best score on five holes and your special playing partner has the best score on four holes during the front nine. You win the $5.00 Nassau bet for the front nine. On the back nine, your special playing partner plays well and wins six of the holes, you win two, and the two of you tie on one hole. Your special playing partner wins the $5.00 Nassau for the back nine. The last Nassau bet is for all eighteen holes. Overall, you won seven holes, and your special playing partner won ten holes, so your special playing partner wins the Nassau bet of $5.00 for the entire round. The result is you owe your special playing partner $5.00 because you won $5.00 from your special playing partner while your special playing partner won $10.00 from you, leaving you owing a net $5.00.

A Nassau bet also has a special option referred to as a press, which starts a new Nassau bet at the point it is initiated and accepted by the golfers in the bet. The press can be called by a golfer anytime they get behind by two holes or more on either the front nine or back nine. Let's say your special playing partner won the first two holes of the back nine. You have the option of calling a press and starting a new Nassau bet starting on hole 12. The original back nine Nassau continues, but now you have an additional Nassau bet going on in addition. The press can turn a low-stakes bet into a high-stakes bet very quickly because each press is a new bet of the designated amount. That means what started as a $5.00 Nassau bet becomes a $10.00 bet with the first push and a $15.00 bet with the second push and so on.

You need to be mindful when and how you introduce betting into the golfing experience with your special playing partner. The prospect of winning or losing money changes the dynamics of the golfing experience and adds an element that can potentially be distracting to developing a relationship and networking with your special playing partner. Thus, you should only introduce betting into the golfing experience if your special playing partner asks to do so and you feel comfortable doing so. If you don't feel comfortable with betting, you can respond to your special playing partner's request by suggesting something like, "I appreciate the invitation, but I was hoping we could use this time to just enjoy being on the course and getting to know each other better," which shows your preference for not betting in a respectful manner. If you do accept the invitation, be sure the designated amount being bet is an amount you feel comfortable losing. In general, a small bet is best because if either you or your playing partner loses, it is less likely to create a negative reaction that can dampen the opportunity to network.

Adaptability

Unless the two of you have discussed an invite earlier in the round, there will be uncertainty as to whether your special playing partner will join you at the nineteenth hole. If you wait until the eighteenth hole to discuss it, you need to prepare yourself to adapt to both a positive and negative response. You can respond to an acceptance of your invite by offering to drive the golf cart to your special playing partner's car in the parking lot so they can put away their golf clubs. After dropping your special playing partner off at their car, you can drive to your car and stow away your clubs before driving back to pick up your special playing partner for the return to the clubhouse. Arriving back at the clubhouse, you and your special playing partner will likely want to wash your hands and freshen up in the locker room before heading to the food and beverage area. There is the possibility that the table you had planned to use for socializing with your special playing partner is not available. Don't panic. Simply adapt and take the next closest table to it. That is part of the advantage to preselecting a table ahead of time. Although it may not be available, it still provides you with a reference area in which to look for a table when you finish your round and arrive at the nineteenth hole. There is also the possibility that no tables are available when you arrive, especially if you happen to be playing during a busy time on the course like a weekend. In this case, ask the staff at the course if they have any outside seating you can use.

What should you do if your special playing partner declines your invitation to join you at the nineteenth hole? You'll still be driving your special playing partner to their car if they decline your invitation, but the drive will be very different. It begins by respecting your special playing partner's decision and offering to drive them to their car by saying something like, "Sorry you can't join me in the clubhouse. Let me drive you to your car so you can put away your clubs." As you drive to their car, you need to ask for a follow-up meeting that will provide you with the opportunity to have the conversation you had expressed wanting to have when you made the invite. This is the time to remind your special playing partner of the topic you said you wanted to discuss when they accepted the invitation. Imagine that your special playing partner is an executive at a company you are trying to gain as a customer and that you had mentioned your desire to talk about their production challenges when you invited the person to join you for a round of golf. A statement like, "We never had a chance to talk about your production challenges like we planned to. Do you have time next week for me to stop by your office and discuss them?" will remind your special playing partner of their agreement to discuss the topic and help you get the follow-up meeting because it taps into the preference for consistency. Most individuals have an inherent desire to have their current behaviors and decisions be consistent with prior ones. Furthermore, this desire increases as individuals age.[14] Reminding your special playing partner that they agreed earlier to talk about a topic will help trigger the consistency effect, making it more likely they will accept your request for a follow-up meeting.

You should also have your business card easily accessible so that you can give it to your special playing partner before they leave. It is a good idea to have your social media information like your web address on LinkedIn on your business card in addition to your name, title, and email. Invite your special playing partner to connect with you online so that you have the opportunity for further engagement after the round. Also, this is the point where it is helpful to provide a memento of the event with a small gift. Gift giving can positively impact business relationships because of the principal of reciprocity, which states that people like to repay others for the kind things that they do for them.[15] The giving of a gift is a kind gesture and will likely encourage your special playing partner to repay the gesture by agreeing to a follow-up meeting. The gift does not need to be extravagant. Instead, a ball marker or golf hat from the course you just played is a useful gift for a golfer and a nice reminder to your special playing partner of the shared experience. Paying for the round is also a recommended gift if you made the invite. Our suggestion is to offer to pay and give a tangible gift that will last beyond the round.

The important thing to remember is that you're developing a relationship with your special playing partner, and their decision to leave right after the round does not end your opportunity in this regard. Rather, it simply means that what you had hoped to accomplish at the nineteenth hole will need to be accomplished later in a different setting. It's important to know ahead of time where and when you would like to have a follow-up meeting with your special playing partner. Trying to decide on a location and time and then making the ask just after your special playing partner has turned down your invitation to the nineteenth hole in the short time it will take to drive to their car will be very difficult and likely not end well. Planning for how you may need to adapt at the nineteenth hole will help ensure your success during this leadership moment on the course.

Heading Back to the Office

Spending significant time with a special playing partner on the golf course provides many important benefits for your career from a leadership perspective. The most obvious is that the golfing experience allows you to develop a relationship with leaders inside and outside of your firm. However, there are also additional, possibly less obvious benefits that you also want to make sure you leverage. One of these less obvious benefits is the opportunity to use the golfing experience for continual development of your leadership ability.[1] Practicing mindfulness, adaptability, curiosity, integrity, empowerment, and strategy at each leadership moment on the course provides valuable experience for continual development of these important leadership traits. Capitalizing on this benefit will make you a better leader and help ensure your success in leadership positions you attain through golfing with special playing partners. Another benefit is the opportunity to engage with your special playing partner beyond the golfing event. These follow-up engagements set the stage for the relationship that developed on the golf course between you and your special playing partner to benefit each of you through information sharing, referrals, and other career-related helping behavior.

It can be easy to overlook the importance of making sure the benefits from the golfing experience actually materialize for you once the golf outing is over and you return to your regular routine. Self-reflection after the event is essential if the experience is to further your development as a leader. Taking the right steps in following up is also critical to determine if the networking that took place on the golf course will truly help you in your career. Likewise, validating the return on the time and money invested in the golf outing will help you both appreciate the value of golf for your career and communicate its value to your superiors when they question whether you should be given time and funding for golfing with special playing partners. We now turn to discussing steps you can take in these areas to ensure a maximal benefit from using golf in your leadership career.

The payoff does not always have to be related to someone outside of your firm. Developing a relationship with a special playing partner inside your firm can be very valuable. For example, I worked for a workers' compensation insurance company as the Northern California manager for premium audit early in my career. Premium audit is not the most admired part of the workers' compensation industry because it determines the final bill for a client, which can upset the client and upset the underwriter in the firm that wrote the policy for the client. One commonality between myself and the underwriting manager for my company was a love of golf. I invited the underwriting manager to join me for a round on the golf course, which went well and led to additional rounds in the future. The rapport developed during those rounds laid the foundation for a trusting and mutually beneficial professional relationship that did not characterize the typical relationship between premium audit and underwriting in many workers' compensation companies.

—Eric

Self-Reflection

Self-reflection about golf outings with special playing partners is important for your continual development as a leader. You should debrief soon after returning from the round of golf with a special playing partner to identify your strengths and weaknesses as a leader at each leadership moment on the course. This process should have two dimensions: self-understanding and self-change.[2] The self-understanding aspect of the debriefing activity focuses on learning about yourself as a leader from the experience. It will enable you to develop a sense of self-knowledge about your responses to experiences during the golf outing with your special playing partner. Many things were likely said and done during the several hours in the round of golf. Some went well, and very likely some did not go as hoped. By spending time to gain self-knowledge, you can create personal meaning from the golfing experience that will help you develop as a leader and respond more effectively in your next golf outing with a special playing partner.

What you gain in self-knowledge should involve both the traits important for success during the golfing experience and the moments that required you to demonstrate leadership traits. Focusing on leadership traits, reflect on when you acted with integrity, adaptability, curiosity, mindfulness, empowerment, and strategy during the round. For example, you should self-reflect on whether you were strategic during the round. You had a main goal for the golf outing of networking successfully with your special playing partner. Did that goal guide your actions during the round, or did other goals less related to networking and possibly more related to your golf score take center stage in guiding your actions? Were there particular events that caused you to stray from focusing on your networking goal and more toward focusing on your golf play? Possibly you were playing the best you had ever played during the round and had a chance to score your personal best score. Did this situation cause you to lose sight of why you were golfing in the first place? If so, what does it say about your ability to remain strategic over the long term? You should self-reflect on each of the leadership traits in this manner.

You should also self-reflect on your leadership at each leadership moment on the course. The golfing experience gave you the opportunity to be a leader at the clubhouse, practice area, tee box, fairway, green, and nineteenth hole. Were there particular moments when you performed better as a leader? Were there particular moments when you performed poorly? The tee box is an area where gender-based microaggressions like statements describing the red tees as "the ladies' tees" can occur. Did this situation arise at the tee box? If so, did you act with integrity in responding to it as a woman or acting as an ally as a man? At the tee box, you also had the opportunity to be empowering by choosing a set of tees that put you in a position to focus on networking with your special playing partner. Did you choose an appropriate set of tee markers for the round, or did you play from a set of tee markers that required you to play a version of the course that required all your attention, taking your focus away from networking with your special playing partner? This type of self-reflection should be done for each leadership moment on the course to help you identify your leadership strengths. It will also allow you to identify areas in need of development from a leadership perspective.

The process you follow in your self-reflection is important and should be characterized as active, persistent, and involving careful consideration. Active self-reflection involves four steps.[3] First, identify and describe subjects to focus on in your self-reflection, including events, people, and actions. Think about each leadership moment and what happened during your time in that moment, focusing on identifying both positive and negative experiences. What events stand out to you from a networking and a playing perspective? Who was involved in these events, and what did they do or not do that stands out? Maybe something negative happened at one of the greens. Did you walk through your special playing partner's line on the green by mistake, or did you let your emotions in response to a poor shot result in a negative experience for your special playing partner? On the positive side, did your group complete the round in a timely manner, or did you and your special playing partner have an in-depth conversation about the topic you wanted to discuss when you made the invitation? Identify who was involved and their part in the event. This could be yourself, your special playing partner, or other golfers in your group. It could be staff from the course like the attendant in the pro shop or someone on the groundskeeping crew. In addition to isolated events, you should also identify general trends that occurred during the golf round. Were you or other golfers regularly slowing down pace of play with errant shots or a lack of attention to the playing order?

The next step requires you to question why the events and actions you identified in the first stage happened as they did during the round. Can you credit the in-depth conversation with your special playing partner to anything you or they did before or during the conversation? Did something come up in your small talk during the round that made it easier to have a conversation after the round at the nineteenth hole? For the negative example, what could have caused you to mistakenly walk in your special playing partner's line? Can you offer any explanation for your action? Is it possible that you got so focused on your own putt that you forgot the position of everyone else's ball on the green or at least the position of the ball for your special playing partner whose line you stepped on? Alternatively, were you too focused on your score and let that contribute to your frustration and negative emotional reaction?

You should give special attention to possible leadership causes for events and actions because an important purpose of self-reflection is development of your leadership ability. The act of stepping on your special playing partner's line was disempowering to them because your steps impacted the ground over which they planned to putt. Maybe this event occurred because you did not practice mindfulness well in getting to the green and you stepped on your special playing partner's line when rushing to your ball to catch up with everyone else. The key is to identify all possible explanations for why an event or action occurred during the golfing experience, especially explanations related to leadership traits that may need further development.

The third stage of the self-reflection process involves identifying ways you can use the positive and improve on the negative experiences from the golf outing. Maybe the good conversation after the round was partly due to you joking around in a positive way with your special playing partner when they arrived at the clubhouse, which set a positive tone for the entire round and afterward. Returning to the event of stepping on your special playing partner's putting line, one way you could have responded differently to your slow play was by offering to have your special playing partner or another golfer in the group go ahead and putt rather than wait on you. This choice would have allowed you to make up for your lack of mindfulness related to pace of play by acting with integrity related to the order of play. This example highlights the importance of considering alternatives related to acting with leadership in ways that would have led to a better reaction on your part. This approach of focusing on how you use the positive experiences and improve on the negative will help you see new opportunities in the future and reflect on areas where your leadership needs work.

Lastly, you should combine what you have learned through the first three stages into a plan of action for the future. Learning from the putting line event, you could plan in the future to act with integrity and offer others the opportunity to play if your pace of play has fallen behind rather than try to rush to make up for the situation. You might also consider apologizing to your special playing partner in a follow-up communication if you caused them to miss an important putt by stepping on their putting line and did not apologize at the time it happened. You don't need to act on all identified events. A cost-benefit analysis will help you identify when to act and when not too. A follow-up apology may not be needed if your special playing partner indicated at the time of the event that they were not bothered by your action. However, a cost-benefit analysis may suggest you should take golf lessons to improve a part of your game that causes your pace of play to be slower than it should be during the round. Doing so will improve your ability to act with mindfulness.

Persistence in your self-reflection is important if the self-reflecting process is to contribute to your development as a leader. It can be easy to choose not to go through the self-reflection process because of distractions or other commitments that grab your attention after the round. You may attempt to self-reflect but do it so quickly that you overlook important events. Not self-reflecting or not giving adequate time to it greatly diminishes the value of the golfing experience for your leadership development. You should give yourself sufficient time to go through the four stages of self-reflection so you do not overlook key events or actions that suggest areas of leadership improvement for yourself. Research suggests allocating fifteen minutes to self-reflection can be sufficient for you to see improvements in your leadership ability.[4] Thus, a long time is not necessarily needed, but you do need to be persistent in allocating sufficient time to learning about your leadership from a golfing experience.

The way you practice self-reflection is also important. Common ways to perform self-reflection include thinking, writing, or talking about events and actions associated with a golfing experience. Thinking involves privately going through the four stages of self-reflection in your mind. Writing and talking are more physically active approaches whereby you write about actions and events in a journal or speak about them into a voice recorder. Research suggests thinking is best when reflecting on positive actions and events, whereas writing and speaking are better ways to self-reflect on negative events and actions.[5] Self-reflection based on thinking is less effective when considering negative events because of the tendency to ruminate and continually generate negative and distracting thoughts rather than viewing the events critically and unbiasedly.[6] Individuals are less prone to ruminate when writing and speaking, making these approaches to self-reflection more effective when evaluating negative experiences.

An important focus of the self-reflection recommended after a golfing experience should be developing your leadership abilities by identifying areas where you can improve. Benefiting from the negative events and actions associated with the golfing experience will require a writing or speaking form of self-reflection to be most useful. Writing and speaking also have the advantage of being more structured ways of reflecting than thinking because grammar in writing and syntax in speech help organize your thoughts and structure them in a way that can help with analyzing the experiences and finding solutions.[7] Whether you choose to use writing or speaking will be a personal preference. You may enjoy putting your thoughts down on paper and the opportunity to reread them as you go through the stages of self-reflection. Alternatively, you may enjoy talking into a voice recorder as if you were speaking to a friend and having the opportunity to relisten to what you said. It is also helpful to talk with someone else (someone you can trust and who has maybe played more golf) to get an extra opinion or recognize something else you missed in your self-reflection. Another option is to practice on the side with your trusted people so they can see you in action, which will help with self-reflection later. Find what works best for you, and you will maximize the learning you gain from self-reflecting on the golfing experience.

The objective behind self-reflection is to recognize the strengths and weaknesses of your leadership. Leveraging your strengths and improving your weaknesses will help you capitalize even more on future opportunities. With respect to weaknesses, the challenges you will face during leadership moments on the course will often be driven by the challenges associated with playing the game of golf. Golf lessons are one way you can improve your ability to play golf, enhancing your ability to be a better leader on the golf course. Almost 20 percent of all golfers take lessons, and there is a $1 billion industry devoted to providing golf instruction.[8] Both the PGA and LPGA certify golf instructors, with over 29,000 PGA professionals and 1,800 LPGA professionals certified by their respective organizations as golf instructors. Both PGA and LPGA professionals must pass a playing ability test and gain hands-on experience teaching golf. In addition, they receive extensive education on various aspects of golf and golf instruction.[9] PGA and LPGA certification is granted once a student passes a series of tests demonstrating their experience and knowledge.

You can purchase a single lesson or a series of lessons depending on what you want to improve and how much development you seek. Ideally, you would do this before playing to get professional advice on how to play on the course and the proper technique for the tee time. A lesson after the round might be appropriate if you only need to tweak a small part of your game, like your grip or alignment. However, a series of lessons will be more appropriate if you are having trouble with several aspects of your game. The cost of golf lessons depends on several factors, including the experience of the professional instructor, the length of the lessons, and the customized nature of the lessons. As with most professionals, a more experienced instructor will cost more, but you may be able to take fewer lessons than if you take lessons from a less experienced golfer. The length of the lessons also matters. Golf lessons are offered in hour-long sessions or increments of an hour like thirty or forty-five minutes. You can expect to pay $75 and above for an hour lesson or $25 and above for a thirty- or forty-five-minute lesson.[10] These are only suggested ranges, and you should confirm with the professional you are considering about their exact rates for golf instruction. The price can also vary based on whether the lessons are individual lessons customized for you or group lessons following a more standardized curriculum. Group lessons will be approximately two-thirds of the cost of individually customized lessons.[11]

Both the PGA and LPGA maintain online directories of certified professionals whom you can contact for golf lessons. You will also find certified professionals working at almost any golf course you play. You can ask in the pro shop if a golf professional is available to provide instruction. A more expensive but also more intensive option is to attend a golf academy. You simply need to enroll in an academy and go through their golf instruction curriculum with the academy instructors. Lastly, there are industry initiatives that offer golf instruction like We Are Golf and Golf 101. We Are Golf is a coalition of industry representatives who have come together to grow the game of golf by providing opportunities for people to learn how to play the game. Golf 101 is an initiative run by the LPGA that offers a standardized curriculum designed for people new to golf and a list of instructors who have been trained in working with beginning golfers.

Follow-Up

It is important to follow up on the golfing experience with your special playing partner in several ways. One of your first actions should be to send a thank-you note to the individual. The note will serve as an additional source of positive reinforcement that can influence your special playing partner's evaluation of their participation in the outing with you. In the note, acknowledge the time your special playing partner gave to the golfing experience. Time is a very valuable resource, and the golfing experience likely took four to five hours. The time your special playing partner gave to the golfing experience is, thus, not inconsequential and should be recognized in your note. You can also recall special positive moments during the golfing experience like a great shot or score by your special playing partner.

Research on the use of acknowledgments, like a thank-you note, suggests they serve many purposes.[12] First, the note will further remind your special playing partner of the relationship between the two of you. This effect is likely to occur most strongly in newly forming relationships, meaning that it is especially important to send a note if the special playing partner is someone you have not known for a long time. In addition to further strengthening the relationship, research suggests that sending a note will magnify positive perceptions and lessen any negative perceptions by your special playing partner. Equally important to remember is that not sending a note can have the opposite effect, making negative experiences be perceived as more negative and reducing perceptions related to positive events.

You should also share any pictures that you took with your special playing partner during the golfing experience. Taking a picture with your special playing partner is good practice during a golf outing and can have a couple of benefits. First, it can help your special playing partner remember the golfing experience, according to research demonstrating that taking a selfie helps individuals remember places they have visited in the past.[13] Each leadership moment represents a place on the course to remember. Taking selfies with your special playing partner at the various leadership moments and then sharing them with the person will improve their memory of leadership moments and the shared experiences you created. Helping your special playing partner remember the event and the shared experiences will serve to strengthen the relationship between the two of you by highlighting your commonalities, enhancing the emergence of trust in your relationship.[14]

Second, taking selfies with your special playing partner during the golfing experience can enhance perceptions of you by others. Research on selfies indicates that how someone is perceived in a selfie is influenced by others in the selfie. Presumably, your special playing partner is a leader in an organization, and being seen with this leader in a selfie can promote positive perception of you as a leader if the special playing partner is viewed positively by others.[15] This effect occurs because the special playing partner serves as a social cue that others use in forming their perceptions of you. Hence, taking selfies with your special playing partner during the golf experience can help develop a relationship with the person and help you be perceived as a leader through your association with them.

However, you should be cautious when sharing pictures taken during a golfing experience. You may be tempted to immediately share the pictures on social media. This can be dangerous for the relationship. It is best to get your special playing partner's permission before sharing pictures of them at the golfing experience online because you do not know the circumstances of their attendance. It is best to share the pictures individually with the person first. In the process, you can ask if they are comfortable with you sharing one or two of the pictures on your social media. Approaching them first before sharing online shows you respect their privacy, which will enhance their trust in you and advance your relationship.[16] Thus, don't be in a rush to post pictures of you with your special playing partner online. It is better to get their permission first before posting.

It is also important to confirm social media connections between you and your special playing partner when sending them a thank-you note and sharing pictures from the golfing experience. You asked them to connect with you on social media at the nineteenth hole. Check if they've done so before you send a note or pictures and remind them to connect if they haven't already. This connection will be important in the future because it provides a channel for communicating with them after the golf outing. People change jobs over time, and your special playing partner may move to another firm. You'll need a way to stay in contact with them if they happen not to send you their email at a new firm. A social media connection allows you to stay in contact no matter what career changes happen to your special playing partner. It also allows you to share your career experiences online. The information you share online will keep your special playing partner updated and potentially serve as a reason for them to contact you when they need information or have information that might benefit you. Social media also enables you to gain insight into the relationship. Your special playing partner liking or commenting on your posts conveys that they view you and their relationship with you positively and are staying engaged in the relationship through social media. It is also a good idea to tag them in relevant posts if they say it is okay. This way, depending on the social media outlet, it will also appear on their feed and their network will notice you.

You will also need to follow up on invitations made during the golfing experience. You should have invited your special playing partner for a follow-up engagement like meeting for a cup of coffee to discuss a possible promotion or visiting their office to discuss them becoming a customer of your firm. Whatever the situation may be, be sure to follow through on your invitation. During the meeting, start to model the types of behaviors you desire from the relationship. As an example, you might make a referral to your special playing partner if you know they have a need and you can't help them but know someone who can. You can also model the flow of information you hope to take place in the relationship by sharing information you have that may be of benefit to your special playing partner. Through your modeling, they will be more inclined to reciprocate and make referrals that benefit you.[17]

ROI Measurement

One of the benefits of using golf to network with leaders is development of your leadership ability based on the experiences from the golf outing. This benefit is important for your career development and should be included in the discussion when determining the return on investment, or ROI, of a golf outing. To illustrate, suppose that it costs $200 to host your special playing partner for a round of golf when you include the green fees, food and beverage, and a small gift. Through self-reflection after the golfing experience, you learned what areas are your strengths and weaknesses from a leadership perspective and created a plan for self-development in leadership areas needing improvement. As an alternative, you could have attended a leadership development class offered by a qualified instructor at a local college or university. The average cost for this type of classroom training ranges from $1,500 to $4,000.[18] Granted, leadership self-development is not a perfect substitute for leadership training offered by qualified instructors. However, it is a valid form of leadership development and one that can be pursued in a cost-effective manner through golfing experiences with special playing partners.

The golfing experience's impact on your development as a leader represents its human resource effect on enhancing your skills.[19] Additionally, the leadership development of golf provides benefits that go beyond your individual development as a leader to impact various aspects of your firm. For example, the strength of a firm's leaders is linked with positive financial outcomes, such as higher sales and enhanced firm performance in areas that contribute to high levels of financial success, like innovation.[20] Second, the leadership development that happens through golfing experiences with special playing partners also has an economic impact through savings on leadership development costs. The $200 it may cost to host a special playing partner for a round of golf is much less than the $1,000 that 70 percent of firms spend, on average, for employee leadership development training.[21] Thus, the use of golf for networking with special playing partners economically impacts a firm through both enhanced financial performance and lower financial costs for leadership development.

The leadership development benefit is important but is not the only benefit to consider when examining the ROI of your golfing experience with a special playing partner. Another benefit is the social resources the golfing experience creates for you. Social resources refer to the relationships you have with others and how these relationships enhance your ability to accomplish goals and objectives.[22] A primary objective of your golf outing was to nurture a relationship with your special playing partner. During the round, you developed the relationship by acting strategically and with integrity, curiosity, empowerment, adaptability, and mindfulness. That relationship is now a resource for you, and the benefits it provides can be calculated against the time and cost of the round.

Good decisions are based on good information. Having nurtured a stronger relationship during the round, you are now in a better position to reach out to your special playing partner when seeking information that can help you access leadership opportunities. As an example, you may be a salesperson and learn about a large international firm opening a manufacturing operation in your town. One of your special playing partners in the past happened to be a member of the local chamber of commerce. The relationship you developed with the person through spending time on the golf course puts you in a better position to contact them and ask what they know about the new international firm and its plans for the manufacturing operation it is opening in town.

Another benefit is the influence you gain through relationships. Continuing with the example, the international firm will need suppliers to help build and run the manufacturing plant it is opening. It is also likely to become active in the local chamber of commerce, creating opportunities for leaders from the international company to interact with your special playing partner. Your special playing partner is likely to refer leaders of the international company to you as a potential supplier because you took the time to develop a relationship with the special playing partner on the golf course. This type of referral can significantly help you in your career by creating opportunities to network with other leaders.

The increased access to information and influence provided by special playing partners has both short-term and long-term benefits. In the short term, they can help you as you go from entry-level to managerial positions. In the long term, they can be beneficial as you move into executive leadership positions. For example, much of your success as a manager will depend upon the quality of people you surround yourself with through hiring decisions. Your network of special playing partners can help you identify potential employees and evaluate applicants. By assisting you in making good hiring decisions, the investments you made in developing relationships with special playing partners in the past will offer benefits far into the future that will enable you to succeed as a manager and rise to executive leadership positions. These types of career benefits are an important reason why over 80 percent of executives say that golf has helped them advance their career.[23]

Relationships with special playing partners can also help you achieve executive leadership positions outside of your company. This is especially true for women, according to research indicating that female golfers have a 54 percent higher likelihood of serving on a board than their male counterparts who play golf.[24] Similarly, people of color who play golf experience greater social mobility in their careers.[25] The same research also suggests that golfing with special playing partners enables women to greatly increase the likelihood of being appointed to the board of a large firm and being appointed to an executive leadership position in male-dominated industries. Through the enhanced access to leadership that golfing provides, new networking opportunities will arise that can further enhance your access to information and influence,[26] increase the likelihood you will acquire CEO positions, and provide you with higher earnings during your career.[27]

Importantly, the type of golf event you and your special playing partner attend during a golf outing can impact the benefits associated with the golfing experience. Inviting your special playing partner to a charity event can create goodwill toward your firm because your participation as an employee signals that your firm supports the cause of the charity. This effect is even better if the special playing partner is a customer or potential customer. More and more customers are using a firm's social impact as a criterion when making a purchase decision.[28] Hosting a leader from a potential customer at a charitable golf event can help build goodwill with that customer and other potential customers you meet at the event. Goodwill extends beyond customers to also impact a firm's ability to recruit good employees, based on research indicating that social impact is becoming more and more important when individuals decide which firms to apply to and join as employees.[29]

Keeping an inventory of the short-term and long-term benefits of golfing with special playing partners is important, especially if you are seeking to have the outings covered by your employer. Individuals who do not play golf will have a hard time appreciating the many benefits that come from golfing with special playing partners and how it can have an important impact on your performance as an employee and the firm's performance. This lack of understanding can serve as a significant barrier to obtaining approval for the time and money needed for golf outings. Thus, it is important for you to share the benefits you gain from golfing experiences with individuals in your firm who have control over resources that can be used to fund this type of professional outing. You can share stories of the benefits you experience when submitting a request for funding a golfing outing. You can also keep mementos of golfing experiences in your office for others to see and ask questions about. A picture of you on the course with a customer or a civic leader highlights the role of golfing experiences in your career success, making your next request for funding to cover an outing less likely to encounter resistance.

The Next Invite

The use of golf experiences with special playing partners to build your social network and access leadership is not a one-time event but should be part of a long-term effort to pursue leadership opportunities. Thus, any individual invite is part of a larger, ongoing process to get yourself invited to golfing experiences by special playing partners and to make invites of special playing partners over the course of your career. You can take certain actions to get yourself invited by a special playing partner to a golfing experience. The first is to be good at your profession. Nothing will make up for not being good at your job. You also need to make it known that you are a golfer. Less than 40 percent of golfers are women,[30] and less than 25 percent are people of color.[31] Thus, others are not likely to automatically think you are a golfer, especially if you are a woman, a person of color, or both. It is important that you address this issue, and you can let people know you are a golfer in many ways. The first action you can take is to use the language of golf at work. Imagine you are giving a presentation to the leadership team at your company. Having given your presentation and answered questions, you can casually announce, "I'm off the tee box. Who's up next?" as you leave the stage and make way for the next speaker. Golfers in the room will immediately pick up on the golfing term "tee box" and start to associate you with golf. Similarly, watch golf events on television and bring them up when you're sitting around a table waiting for a meeting with leaders in your company to begin. Asking if anyone watched a televised golf tournament over the weekend will signal you are a golfer to those around the table and increase the likelihood your name will come to mind next time someone is needed for a golf outing with a client or at a charity event hosted by your company. The most watched golf tournaments are the major events for men and women professional golfers. Watching those events when they're on television will provide you with the events and language to use at work in letting people know you golf.

Another action you can take is to display golf-related pictures and items in your office at work. These can be pictures of courses you've played or desire to play. They can be pictures of you and special playing partners at past golfing experiences. Framed golf flags are also good items because they're large, making their presence on the wall very noticeable. Having a putter and ball in your office can also be a strong signal to others that you golf. It's likely that other golfers who see the putter will want to pick it up and hit a few putts on the carpet. They may ask you about your putting game and your golf interest in general. Don't be surprised to hear, "I didn't know you were a golfer." Seize on this type of situation when it occurs by talking about your golf interest and asking the person whether they play. These exchanges plant a seed in the mind of other golfers that can result in you being invited to a golfing experience with leaders in your firm.

The clothes you wear can also be used to signal to others that you play golf. A collared shirt with the logo of a golf course you've played lets people you come across know that you have an interest in golf. Even better, wear a shirt from a prior golfing experience with a special playing partner. Wearing a golf hat with the logo of a course you've played can act in a similar way, increasing the chances you will be considered by leaders in your firm for a golf invite.

In addition to promoting your golf interest inside your firm with potential special playing partners, you should also continue to nurture your relationship with special playing partners from the past. A completed golfing experience is a milestone but not the end of your networking with a special playing partner. Regular interaction helps develop fondness between you and your special playing partner that can promote greater trust in your relationship.[32] In turn, the trust that develops between you and your special playing partner promotes commitment by each of you to the relationship and increases the likelihood your special playing partner will cooperate when you ask for information or assistance in the future.[33] At the same time, you need to be sensitive to respond favorably to requests for information and assistance from your special playing partners. The emergence of a strong relationship that is based on trust and commitment requires both parties to act in ways beneficial to the relationship. This means that you can't just be a taker, always asking for help but not willing to provide help when asked for it in return. Thus, be willing to help your special playing partner when they inevitably ask for your assistance. It is advisable to go beyond waiting to be asked for help by your special playing partner and be proactive in providing them with help. Proactively seeking ways to help your special playing partners positions you as someone who is voluntarily looking out for their interests and trying to help them be successful. This will be seen as a form of altruism or benevolence by your partner and help strengthen the relationship between you.

You should also be looking for your next special playing partner after having completed a golfing experience. Increasing the size of your network or the number of people you know and have some form of relationship with is important because a large network can provide you with social benefits like increased prominence in the eyes of others because of who you know. In addition to fostering a large network, you also want to build a network that is broad in the sense that it involves relationships between you and people from different backgrounds, experiences, jobs, and other areas of professional employment. A broad network will provide access to more diverse information and resources that can provide you with more options when seeking assistance.[34] Thus, good networking is a never-ending process because of the benefits a large and broad network can provide you during your career.

Creating a broad network requires you to carefully consider whom you add to your network. You want people who have varied experiences and hold different positions as special playing partners. You also want people with different positions and who come from different industries. It can be easy to network with the same type of people. In fact, research shows that our natural tendency is to connect with people who are like us.[35] However, a broad network that will be able to help you across a variety of situations and bring to you a variety of leadership opportunities requires that you connect with people who differ from you and from each other.

Participating in professional and civic groups is one way you can meet new and varied people who are potential special playing partners. Joining a golf league or other sport group is another way. Continue building your network by consistently inviting new special playing partners for golfing experiences. By ensuring that each next special playing partner adds to both the size and breadth of your network, you will build a network that will be helpful to you across a myriad of situations that can arise over the course of your leadership career.

Leadership and Golf for Life

Demonstrating leadership is an important skill for success whether you're on the golf course or back at the office. Preparation and ongoing investment in leadership development can help you be a more effective leader in both situations. This book focused on six traits that are required to be a good leader: adaptability, curiosity, empowerment, integrity, mindfulness, and strategy. A good leader adapts to changing circumstances, pivoting in the moment to a more effective strategy. Curiosity captures the importance of information and the need to ask questions and gather information before acting. Empowerment ensures that you act with autonomy and help others do the same. Integrity involves acting in a way that is respectful to yourself and others. Mindfulness is the need to be present and focused on what is happening to you in a moment rather than replaying the past or rehearsing the future. Not every decision will turn out as hoped. Therefore, a good leader adapts by thinking through strategic approaches for achieving their goals.

The discussion also identified key leadership moments on the golf course requiring each of the leadership traits, starting with the clubhouse where the golfing experience with your special playing partner begins. Leadership is also required at the practice area where you prepare yourself to play and initiate the relationship development process with your special playing partner. The tee box provides many challenges each time you start playing one of the eighteen holes in a round of golf. The leadership moments on the fairway present many opportunities for nurturing the relationship with your special playing partner but also challenges that can become obstacles to the relationship. The discussion also described the green as a leadership moment. Lastly, the nineteenth hole is where the golfing experience hopefully ends and provides an opportunity for socializing with your special playing partner about the leadership goal that motivated you to ask them to join you for a round of golf. However, like the other leadership moments, the nineteenth hole presents both opportunities and challenges that must be managed successfully.

Put Leadership Lessons into Practice

From a strategic perspective, it is important to remember the importance of having goals for the golfing experience and letting them guide you at each leadership moment. The overarching goal is to use the golfing experience to expand your social network of professional contacts whom you can draw upon when accessing leadership opportunities. Each leadership moment presents an opportunity for you to achieve objectives toward this goal, ranging from having your special playing partner start engaging with you at the practice area at the beginning of the round to spending time socializing at the nineteenth hole at the end of the round. In between, the objective is to build rapport, advance trust, and develop commitment between you and your special playing partner.

The discussion highlighted the need to be mindful of microaggressions that can occur on the golf course. Women and people of color can face bias that others may not experience. Real examples of being mistaken for a caddy or server working at the course rather than someone there to play a round of golf can negatively impact the outcome of a round with a special playing partner. It is also common to hear microaggressions at the tee box when someone suggests a certain set or color of tee markers is for women and implies all the other tees are for men. The discussion also identified ways of handling these moments through tactics that allow you to navigate an authentic response. The goal is to ensure they do not become a distraction and obstacle to using the golf experience to effectively access leaders and leadership opportunities.

Acting with empowerment involves making decisions that allow you to use the golfing experience to develop a relationship with your special playing partner. Some of the decisions are logistical, like setting a place with your special playing partner for the two of you to meet at the clubhouse when starting the golfing experience. Others are more related to playing decisions; for example, choosing a set of tees to play at the tee box that offers a level of difficulty that allows you to focus more on engaging with your special playing partner and less on your golf play for the round. Empowerment also involves allowing your special playing partner to be at their best on the golf course through actions like repairing divots on the green. The discussion also revealed the value of using humor in diffusing the negative emotional experiences that inevitably accompany playing a difficult game like golf so they do not become an obstacle to creating a positive golfing experience each of you will enjoy as you develop a relationship.

Lessons about being mindful focused on distinguishing between different topics of small talk and using your knowledge of where you are on the golf course at any point in time to know the appropriate topics to discuss. It is good to start the round with golf-related small talk before moving to more personal small talk allowing self-disclosure by your special playing partner. This means that business talk should not be the focus of small talk until you arrive at the nineteenth hole. However, this can change if your special playing partner brings up business during the round. Mindfulness is also useful for dealing with uncomfortable situations like being stared at on the golf course. It helps you focus on what is important in a moment and allows you to block out uncomfortable and inappropriate staring during a round and keep it from distracting you from accessing leaders and leadership opportunities with golf.

The discussion also revealed the many benefits of curiosity. At the beginning, curiosity enables you to identify if a leader is a golfer and likely to join you for a round of golf. Without this form of curiosity, the golfing experience never happens, and you miss a chance to leverage the professional opportunities golf can provide you in your leadership career. Curiosity is also important in promoting small talk with your special playing partner. The information shared during these informal and abbreviated conversations in the round enables you and your special playing partner to identify common interests, perspectives, and values that will provide the foundation for developing a relationship.

Lastly, adaptability comes into play at several points. You adapt your course selection for the round based on the playing ability and course preferences of your special playing partner. Adaptation also includes adjusting your schedule if you're unable to spend time in the practice area with your special playing partner because they are running late or may not feel the need to warm up. Adaptability also requires aligning your language by matching language or using humor to manage the emotions that arise during the round, especially negative emotions that can derail the golfing experience. Lastly, your special playing partner may decline the invitation to join you at the nineteenth hole. In this case, you need to respond accordingly and use the remaining time before your special playing partner leaves the course to schedule a follow-up meeting after the round where you can discuss the topic that motivated the golf outing.

Getting Ready to Play

The discussion provided several recommendations from a golf-playing perspective, not so much about the technicalities of the swing but more about managing the playing and social aspects at each leadership moment. At the clubhouse, follow golf etiquette and arrive early for your tee time and check with the pro shop about special conditions or special rules for the round. Knowing, for example, if the golf cart rules for the day require you to stay on the cart path is important. You should also get information about pin positions for the round so that you and your special playing partner can effectively determine the distance for shots from the fairway to the green.

The practice area allows you to study your shot pattern. Are you slicing the ball and ending up far right of where you are aiming? If so, then you should aim to the left with your shots during the round. The opposite will be the case if your shots at the practice area are trending toward the left because you are hooking the ball or hitting a draw. Hitting warm-up putts is also important, especially given that putting will account for the greatest percentage of strokes in the round. You'll want to practice lag putts to avoid three-putting greens. Lastly, make sure you have the golf accessories you need for the round, including tees, a ball marker, and golf balls. Your pace of play will be much better if you have these items ready for use during the round.

The discussion reviewed many lessons for the tee box. Most important is choosing the set of tee markers that will enable you to play a challenging version of the course but not so challenging that it distracts from your ability to engage with your special playing partner during the round or causes you to have an especially slow pace of play. Paying attention to the tee signage is also important. The information about hole yardage, the layout of the hole, bunkers, and hazards is essential for making an effective tee shot. You'll also need to consider the format of play. Playing captain's choice rather than a regular round of golf will require you to be less aggressive with your tee shot if your special playing partner has not found the fairway with their tee shot. Alternatively, you can be more aggressive with your tee shot if your playing partners have already landed in the fairway. You also should be mindful of the order of play off the tee box unless your group has decided to play ready golf. Lastly, remember to play a provisional ball from the tee box if there is doubt about whether one of your drives went out of bounds. Doing so will save time by preventing you from having to come back to the tee box and rehit if the ball did go out of bounds.

The fairway requires many golfing decisions, not least of which is choosing your shot from the fairway to the green. The smart shot is not always the shot aimed directly at the hole on the green because there may be several hazards around the green that are difficult to miss with a shot aimed at the hole. A smarter shot in those cases is a shot to the green but away from the hole. The same is true if you miss the fairway and end up in the rough or trees. The smart shot may require you to layup or punch out rather than try to hit directly onto the green. An ever-present issue is the pace of play. Maintain a good pace of play in the fairway by being ready to play when it's your turn and knowing how to handle situations in a timely manner when your ball goes into a hazard or possibly out of bounds.

Another situation that can impact the pace of play in the fairway is when food carts come around on the golf course. The food cart is a golf cart that has been converted into a moving canteen, meaning it will contain food and beverages that you can buy while you're playing and away from the clubhouse. Just as you want to be thinking about your next golf shot before you get to the ball, you also want to be thinking about what you want from the food cart before you arrive at it. Taking a long time at the food cart can slow down the group and negatively impact pace of play. The best advice is to order something you can buy and consume quickly while you're on your way to hit your ball. It's also good etiquette to offer to buy your special playing partner's food and beverage the first time the food cart comes around.

Many rules and etiquette govern play at the green, including order of play, with the player whose ball is farthest away from the hole playing first. The rules provide you with the opportunity to mark your ball on the green and pick it up. This is the first time you can move the ball once it is hit into play off the tee box. However, you must be careful when marking the ball that you don't inadvertently touch it before your marker is in place. The forms of etiquette on the green are many. You should repair any divot your ball creates when it lands on the green and be careful not to step in the putting line of your special playing partner or that of others in your playing group. It's also important to stand out of eyesight of your playing partners when they are putting and avoid any distracting movement or talking when anyone is standing ready to putt their ball.

The discussion also discussed advice for playing at the green in addition to golf rules and etiquette. Effective putting requires avoiding three-putting by ensuring that your first putt stops close to the hole if it does not go into the hole. Sometimes it is helpful to imagine a small circle around the hole within which you want the ball to stop if it misses the hole. Good putting also requires reading the green by studying the speed of the green based on whether you are putting downhill, making the speed faster, or uphill, making the speed slower. The direction the putt will break is also important to know because it will impact the aim of your putt. Lastly, understanding distance is key to knowing how firmly or softly to hit your putt. Combine distance, speed, and direction together and you have your read of the green and the information needed to make a good putt.

Now that you have the basics, how do you continue to develop as a golfer and a leader? Developing solid golf skills requires a commitment to practice. There are several things you can do to set yourself up for ongoing success.

Find a Golf Experience That Fits Your Needs

Playing a round of golf with a special playing partner provides networking opportunities that will have consequences for your career and your ability to help your special playing partner in their career. Sometimes, it can be difficult to get a special playing partner to commit to a full round of golf and the four or more hours it takes to play eighteen holes. This can be true if a special playing partner's job is very demanding and leaves them little time for activities outside of the office. In other situations, your special playing partner may enjoy golf but not feel comfortable enough with their golfing ability to play a full round. You may also feel this way when you are first learning the game. Playing eighteen holes when you are just beginning to play can seem like a daunting task. However, whether the issue is time or playing comfort, it does not eliminate golf from being a way to network with a special playing partner. The challenge is to find a way to have a golfing experience that is not as time consuming or challenging from a playing perspective.

Fortunately, off-course golfing opportunities have recently started to appear that can provide an opportunity to create golfing experiences with special playing partners when you or your partner are unable or unwilling to commit substantial time to networking. Referred to as golfing entertainment, these off-course golf venues include indoor simulators and driving ranges that provide hitting bays and often include food services.[1] One way to think of them is that they provide a combination of the practice area and nineteenth hole and serve as a place to go practice if you want to mix it up or make it more fun.

Like your arrival at a golf course, your visit to an off-course golf venue begins with checking in at the front desk where they assign you a bay to hit balls. However, these bays are not lined up like you would find at a traditional golf course but rather are part of a multilevel complex. Another difference from the practice area at a golf course is that you pay by the hour at these venues and can hit as many balls as you like during your time in the hitting bay. You typically will not be hitting off grass but, instead, you'll be using man-made mats. The hitting bays also provide you with games you can play that allow you to accumulate putts based on your accuracy in hitting balls to targets down range.

You should use the time in the hitting bay to generate small talk with your special playing partner by asking questions about their hobbies, interests, and family. One thing to keep in mind when accessing a golf entertainment center is that you are not preparing to play a round of golf. Thus, several things that are important at the practice area of the golf course are not relevant here. There's no need to ensure you have golf balls, markers, and tees. You also don't need to focus on the flight of your special playing partner's shots, except to offer compliments and use them as the subject for small talk. The point is to use the time hitting balls to begin developing the relationship with your special playing partner similarly to how you would at the practice area before playing a round of golf.

The nineteenth hole aspect of off-course golf venues is the food and beverage service they provide while you're hitting balls in the hitting bay with your special playing partner. Food servers will take your order from a menu of different food and beverage offerings. Like at the nineteenth hole, you should follow your special playing partner's lead before ordering alcohol. Fortunately, you don't need to worry as much about logistical issues at off-course golf venues because each hitting bay area is the same and you will not have other people in yours. Thus, there's no concern about getting a good table like at the nineteenth hole and being situated well for talking with your special playing partner.

The goal you have at the nineteenth hole on the golf course is the same as when you're socializing with your special playing partner at an off-course golf venue. You invited the special playing partner because you wanted to develop a relationship with them and discuss a leadership-related topic like a promotion or gaining their company as a customer. Fortunately, you don't have to worry about them not accepting your invitation to join you at the nineteenth hole like you would during a traditional golfing experience at a golf course. They accepted your invitation to the off-course golfing venue, and now you can speak with them about your professional goal. The informal nature of off-course golf venues makes them ideal for having these types of conversations.

You might worry how your special playing partner will respond to you inviting them to an off-course golf venue rather than to play a round at a golf course. They will welcome the invite if they like golf but are very busy or concerned about their playing ability. This will be especially true of special playing partners just beginning to play golf or those who haven't played in a while who may be concerned about playing poorly. An additional benefit is that you can increase the chances of later playing a regular round of golf with a special playing partner who is new to the game. According to data published by the National Golf Federation, 75 percent of nongolfers said that time spent at an off-course golf venue increased their interest in playing at a traditional golf course.[2] Additionally, 29 percent of them said that playing at an off-course venue increased the amount of golf they played on traditional golf courses.

Bring Others into the Game

Each of your special playing partners invested in you by taking the time to spend a significant amount of time with you during your first golf outing with them. The relationship that the golfing experience sparked will help you gain access to important information and referrals who will help you advance in your leadership career. It is important to demonstrate your gratitude to your special playing partners by being their ally when they approach you for help. It also is important that you express your gratitude by paying forward the benefits you received through golf to others. Paying it forward is a prosocial behavior that is motivated by both a sense of gratitude for how you have benefited from a situation and the desire to help others do the same.[3] It is a more generalized form of reciprocity, which we discussed earlier. However, rather than benefiting yourself from an act of reciprocity, your acts to pay it forward focus not on your special playing partners but on other colleagues who seek leadership opportunities in their career.[4] Think of it as being a good citizen with your efforts to help others like your past special playing partners have helped you in your career.

One way you can pay forward the benefits you receive through the professional network golf helps you create is by being a mentor to junior colleagues. Mentoring is a relational approach to others that focuses on the development of junior colleagues. As you rise in business leadership, you can develop future leaders by inviting younger, less senior individuals either in your firm or in other firms to join you for a golfing experience. Your invite will have several benefits for the rising leader you invite. First, it can reduce a significant barrier to building the type of professional network needed for accessing leadership opportunities, especially for women and people of color. It can be risky for a junior colleague to ask a senior leader to join them for a golfing experience, yet building a professional network of leaders can be extremely helpful in the path to leadership. You can remove the riskiness of asking a senior leader to a golf experience by making the invite yourself. Second, you will be modeling how to make an invite for a golfing experience, which will help a junior colleague when making their own invites in the future. Third, you will be signaling the importance of golfing experiences as a means for accessing leaders, promoting their networking activity in the future.

Equally important, you should accept invites from junior colleagues when they ask you. By accepting an invite to a golf experience from a junior colleague, you can pay forward the benefits you have received from golfing experiences with special playing partners on your way to becoming a leader. In addition to giving them the opportunity to develop a relationship with you, your acceptance also reinforces the value of golfing experiences for accessing leaders, making it more likely they will continue to use the opportunity golfing provides for accessing leadership.

Focusing on junior colleagues when making and accepting invites also pays it forward from a leadership development perspective. You understand the importance of being adaptable, curious, empowering, and mindful and of acting with integrity and thinking strategically. Golfing experiences with junior staff members will allow you to model those leadership behaviors with rising leaders. You can offer advice when one or more of these traits are missing from their behavior. Their absence will be noticeable, and the golfing experience will give you the opportunity to help junior staff members develop as leaders through both your own actions in exhibiting these behaviors and your words of encouragement that help develop them in others.

You've made an important step by reading this book. Now it's time to get out there and play your first round. You have the skills and mindset to show up as a solid leader both on and off the course. Go get started and enjoy the journey.

Notes

Introduction

1. Dawnet Beverley, "Golf as a Tool for Executive Leadership Development" (MA diss., Graziadio Business School, 2014), 449.
2. Paul L. Nesbit, "The Role of Self-Reflection, Emotional Management of Feedback, and Self-Regulation Processes in Self-Directed Leadership Development," *Human Resource Development Review* 11, no. 2 (April 2012): 203–26, https://doi.org/10. 1177/1534484312439196.
3. Kristi Dosh, "Golfers Make Better Business Executives," *Forbes*, May 16, 2016, https://www.forbes.com/sites/kristidosh/2016/05/16/golfers-make-better-business-executives/?sh=3fa97187b4a5.
4. Dosh.
5. Debery Cook, "$4 Billion Generated Annually by Golf Tournament Fundraising," *African American Golfer's Digest*, August 26, 2015, https://africanamerican golfersdigest.com/4-billion-generated-annually-by-golf-tournament-fundraising/.
6. Judith Warner, Nora Ellmann, and Diana Boesch, "The Women's Leadership Gap," *Center for American Progress*, November 20, 2018, https://www.americanprogress. org/issues/women/reports/2018/11/20/461273/womens-leadership-gap-2/.
7. Warner, Ellmann, and Boesch.
8. Khristopher J. Brooks, "Why So Many Black Business Professionals Are Missing from the C-Suite," *CBS News*, December 10, 2019, https://www.cbsnews.com/news/ black-professionals-hold-only-3-percent-of-executive-jobs-1-percent-of-ceo-jobs-at-fortune-500-firms-new-report-says/.
9. J. D. Swerzenski, Donald Tomaskovic, and Eric Hoyt, "This Is Where There Are the Most Hispanic Executives (and It's Not Where You Think)," *Fast Company*, January 28, 2020, https://www.fastcompany.com/90456329/this-is-where-there-are-the-most-hispanic-executives-and-its-not-where-you-think.
10. Warner, Ellmann, and Boesch.
11. "Golf Industry Facts," National Golf Foundation, accessed July 18, 2021, https:// www.ngf.org/golf-industry-research/.

12. Michael McCann, "Why Private Golf Clubs Are Legally Still Able to Discriminate Against Women," *Sports Illustrated*, July 1, 2019, https://www.si.com/golf-archives/2019/07/01/private-golf-clubs-muirfield-augusta-women-discrimination.

13. Lee McGinnis, Julia McQuillan, and Constance L. Chapple, "I Just Want to Play: Women, Sexism, and Persistence in Golf," *Journal of Sport & Social Issues* 29, no. 3 (August 2005): 313–37, https://doi.org/10.1177/0193723504272659.

14. John Fry and Philip Hall, *Women's, Girls' and Family Participation in Golf: An Overview of Existing Research*, R&A, accessed July 18, 2021, https://www.walesgolf.org/wp-content/uploads/2018/02/RA-Research-doc-FULL-1.pdf.

15. Jeff Stone, Christian I. Lynch, Mike Sjomeling, and John M. Darley, "Stereotype Threat Effects on Black and White Athletic Performance," *Journal of Personality and Social Psychology* 77, no. 2 (June): 1213–27, https://doi.org/10.1037/0022-3514.77.6.1213.

16. "How Much Do Golf Lessons Cost?" Back 2 Basics Golf, October 13, 2020, https://back2basics.golf/blogs/news/how-much-do-golf-lessons-cost.

17. Philip Delves Broughton, "The Busiest Executives Still Find Time for a Round of Golf," *Financial Times*, August 27, 2012, https://www.ft.com/content/ab03b6e0-ee1f-11e1-a9d7-00144feab49a.

18. Francesca Gino, "The Business Case for Curiosity," *Harvard Business Review* 96 (September–October 2018): 48–57, https://hbr.org/2018/09/the-business-case-for-curiosity.

19. Spencer Harrison, Erin Pinkus, and John Cohen, "Research: 83% of Executives Say They Encourage Curiosity. Just 52% of Employees Agree," *Harvard Business Review*, September 20, 2018, https://hbr.org/2018/09/research-83-of-executives-say-they-encourage-curiosity-just-52-of-employees-agree.

20. Harrison, Pinkus, and Cohen.

21. Martin Reeves and Mike Deimler, "Adaptability: The New Competitive Advantage," *Harvard Business Review* 89 no. 7/8 (July–August 2011): 131–141, https://hbr.org/2011/07/adaptability-the-new-competitive-advantage.

22. Amy Walters, "Adaptability Skills in the Workplace," EY, accessed July 18, 2021, https://www.lane4performance.com/insight/blog/importance-of-adaptability-skills-in-the-workplace/.

23. Allan Lee, Sara Willis, and Amy Wei Tian, "When Empowering Employees Works, and When It Doesn't," *Harvard Business Review*, March 2, 2018, https://hbr.org/2018/03/when-empowering-employees-works-and-when-it-doesnt.

24. "Why Empowering Employees is an Important Facet of Leadership," Advanced Leadership Consulting, accessed July 18, 2021, http://leadershipconsulting.com/why-empowering-employees-is-an-important-facet-of-leadership/.

25. Terri Williams, "Why Integrity Remains One of the Top Leadership Attributes," *Economist*, accessed July 18, 2021, https://execed.economist.com/blog/industry-trends/why-integrity-remains-one-top-leadership-attributes.

26. Williams.

27. Lynn Sharp Paine, "Managing for Organizational Integrity," *Harvard Business Review* 72, no. 2 (March/April 1994): 106–17, https://hbr.org/1994/03/managing-for-organizational-integrity.

28. Marissa Levin, "Harvard Research Reveals How Mindful Leaders Develop Better Companies and Happier Employees," *Inc.*, February 28, 2018, https://www.inc.com/marissa-levin/harvard-research-reveals-how-mindful-leaders-develop-better-companies-happier-employees.html.

29. Alison Beard, "Mindfulness in the Age of Complexity," *Harvard Business Review* 92, no. 3 (March 2014): 68–73, https://hbr.org/2014/03/mindfulness-in-the-age-of-complexity.

30. Cynthia A. Montgomery, "Putting Leadership Back into Strategy," *Harvard Business Review* 86, no. 1 (January 2008): 54–60, https://hbr.org/2008/01/putting-leadership-back-into-strategy.

31. Bernardo Silva, Wayne Nelson, Tom Schoenwaelder, and Sarit Markivitch, "2020 Chief Strategy Officer Survey," Deloitte, April 16, 2020, https://www2.deloitte.com/us/en/insights/topics/leadership/chief-strategy-officer-survey.html.

1. Golf 101

1. Joel Beal, "How Far Do Average Golfers *Really* Hit It? New Distance Data Will Surprise You," *Golf Digest*, January 4, 2017, https://www.golfdigest.com/story/how-far-do-average-golfers-really-hit-it-new-distance-data-will-surprise-you.

2. Jesse Penn, interview conducted by Eric Boyd, December 20, 2020.

3. *NGF Golf Instruction Report Overview*, National Golf Foundation, accessed July 18, 2021, https://www.ngf.org/ngf-releases-golf-instruction-report/.

4. Tiger Woods, *How I Play Golf* (New York: Grand Central Publishing, 2011).

5. Brent Kelley, "Ben Hogan Quotes: Best Sayings by and about the Golfer," liveaboutdotcom, updated on November 03, 2018, https://www.liveabout.com/ben-hogan-quotes-1563658.

2. Leadership at the Clubhouse

1. David Taylor, "The New World of the PGA Assistant Professional," *Golf Monthly*, January 11, 2016, https://www.golfmonthly.com/features/the-game/the-new-world-of-the-pga-assistant-professional-85597.

2. Mitchell Houston, "Michael Jordan Banned from Golf Course for Wearing Cargo Shorts," *Los Angeles Times*, November 29, 2012, https://www.latimes.com/sports/la-xpm-2012-nov-29-la-sp-sn-michael-jordan-banned-20121129-story.html.

3. Francesca Gino, Maryam Kouchaki, and Tiziana Casciaro, "Why Connect? Moral Consequences of Networking with a Promotion or Prevention Focus," *Journal of Personality and Social Psychology* 119, no. 6 (December 2020): 1221–38, https://doi.org/10.1037/pspa0000226.

4. Tiziana Casciaro, Francesca Gino, and Maryam Kouchaki, "Learn to Love Networking," *Harvard Business Review* 94, no. 5 (May 2016): 104–7, https://hbr.org/2016/05/learn-to-love-networking.

5. Anat Stavans and Ronit Webman Shafran, "The Pragmatics of Requests and Refusals in Multilingual Settings," *International Journal of Multilingualism* 15, no. 2 (June 2017): 1–20, https://doi.org/10.1080/14790718.2017.1338708.

6. Chak Fu Lam, Cynthia Lee, and Yang Sui, "Say It as It Is: Consequences of Voice Directness, Voice Politeness, and Voicer Credibility on Voice Endorsement," *Journal of Applied Psychology* 104, no. 5 (May 2019): 642–58, https://doi.org/10.1037/apl0000358.

7. Cass Shum, Anthony R. Gatling, Laura A. Book, and Billy Bai, "The Moderating Roles of Follower Conscientiousness and Agreeableness on the Relationship Between Peer Transparency and Follower Transparency," *Journal of Business Ethics* 154, no. 2 (January 2019): 483–95.

8. David W. Johnson, "Cooperativeness and Social Perspective Taking," *Journal of Personality and Social Psychology* 31, no. 2 (June 1975): 241–44, https://doi.org/10.1037/h0076285.

9. Lawrence Smelser, "Average Golf Score," *Golfible*, last updated on January 19, 2022, https://golfible.com/average-golf-score/.

10. Dean Knuth, "Handicaps - Your Questions Answered," *PopeOfSlope*, accessed July 18, 2021, http://www.popeofslope.com/magazine/aver_rating.html.

11. Robert C. Liden, Sandy J. Wayne, Raymond T. Sparrow, "An Examination of the Mediating Role of Psychological Empowerment on the Relations between the Job, Interpersonal Relationships, and Work Outcomes." *Journal of Applied Psychology* 85, no. 3 (June 2000): 407–16.

12. Fred Alveter, "Golf Generates $3.9 Billion Annually for Charity," *Ohio Golf Journal*, May 13, 2018, https://ohiogolfjournal.com/golf-generates-3-9-billion-annually-for-charity.

13. Michael McCann, "Why Private Golf Clubs are Legally Still Able to Discriminate Against Women," *Sports Illustrated*, July 21, 2019, https://www.si.com/golf-archives/2019/07/01/private-golf-clubs-muirfield-augusta-women-discrimination.

14. "Golf Industry Facts," National Golf Foundation, accessed July 30, 2021, https://www.ngf.org/golf-industry-research/.

15. Michael Palanski, Kristin Cullen, William Gentry, and Chelsea Nichols, "Virtuous Leadership: Exploring the Effects of Leader Courage and Behavioral Integrity on Leader Performance and Image," *Journal of Business Ethics* 132, no. 2 (December 2015): 297–310, https://doi.org/10.1007/s10551-014-2317-2.

16. Patricia Pullin, "Small Talk, Rapport, and Intentional Communication Competence," *Journal of Business Communication* 47, no. 4 (October 2010): 455–76, https://doi.org/10.1177/0021943610377307.

17. Janet Holmes and Maria Stubbe, *Power and Politeness in the Workplace* (New York: Routledge Publishing, 2015).

3. Leadership at the Practice Area

1. Luke Kerr-Dineen, "How Tiger Warms Up: A Minute-by-Minute Breakdown of His Pre-Round Practice Routine," *Golf*, November 30, 2018, https://golf.com/instruction/short-game/tiger-woods-warm-up-practice-routine/.

2. Timo Kaski, Karkko Niemi, and Ellen Pullins, "Rapport Building in Authentic B2B sales Interaction," *Industrial Marketing Management* 69, no. 18 (February 2018): 235–52, https://doi.org/10.1016/j.indmarman.2017.08.019.

3. David Allen, "Bump and Run Suzy Whaley," GOLF Channel, September 11, 2009, https://www.golfchannel.com/article/david-allen/bump-and-run-suzy-whaley.

4. Andrew K. Przybylski and Netta Weinstein, "Can You Connect With Me Now? How the Presence of Mobile Communication Technology Influences Face-to-Face Conversation Quality," *Journal of Social and Personal Relationships* 30, no. 3 (July 2013): 237–46, https://doi.org/10.1177/0265407512453827.

5. Robert B. Cialdini, *Influence, New and Expanded: The Psychology of Persuasion* (New York: Harper Business, 2021).

6. Elaine G. Hatfield, William Walster, and Ellen Berscheid, *Equity: Theory and Research* (Boston: Allyn & Bacon, 1978).

7. Patricia M. Doney and Joseph P. Cannon, "An Examination of the Nature of Trust in Buyer-Seller Relationships," *Journal of Marketing* 61, no. 2 (April 1997): 35–51, https://doi.org/10.2307/1251829.

8. Judith Warner, Nora Ellmann, and Diana Boesch, "The Women's Leadership Gap," Center for American Progress, November 20, 2018, https://www.americanprogress.org/issues/women/reports/2018/11/20/461273/womens-leadership-gap-2/.

9. Doney and Cannon.

10. Derald Wing Sue, *Microaggressions in Everyday Life: Race, Gender, and Sexual Orientation* (John Wiley & Sons Inc., 2010).

11. Derald Wing Sue et al., "Disarming Racial Microaggressions: Microintervention Strategies for Targets, White Allies, and Bystanders," *American Psychologist* 74, no. 1 (January 2019): 128–42.

12. Sue et al.

13. Monnica T. Williams et al., "Reducing Microaggressions and Promoting Interracial Connection: The Racial Harmony Workshop," *Journal of Contextual Behavioral Science* 16, no. 2 (April 2020): 153–61.

14. Carolyn Massiah, interview conducted by Eric Boyd, March 11, 2021.

4. Leadership at the Tee Box

1. "Topic—Starting the Hole (Teeing Area)," United States Golf Association, accessed June 7, 2021, https://www.usga.org/content/usga/home-page/rules-hub/topics/teeing-area.html.

2. Pete McDaniel, *Uneven Lies: The Heroic Story of African-Americans in Golf* (Connecticut: The American Golfer, 2000).

3. Kylie Garabed, "Dr. George Grant and Evolution of the Golf Tee," United States Golf Association, July 3, 2018, https://www.usga.org/content/usga/home-page/articles/2018/07/dr--george-grant-and-evolution-of-the-golf-tee-.html.

4. Bob Denney, "How Dr. George F. Grant Went from African American Dentist to Golf Tee Inventor," Professional Golfers Association of America, February 10, 2018, https://www.pga.com/archive/how-dr-george-f-grant-went-african-american-dentist-golf-tee-inventor.

5. Erinie Lo, "Average Golf Course Length; Size | Acres | Areas," Golf Storage Guide, accessed June 8, 2021, https://www.golfstorageguide.com/golf-course-length-size-acres/.
6. "U.S. Handicapping Statistics," United States Golf Association, accessed June 8, 2021, https://www.usga.org/content/usga/home-page/handicapping/handicapping-stats.html.
7. "PGA and USGA Step to New Sets of Tees in 'Tee It Forward' Initiative," Professional Golfers Association of America, May 24, 2011, https://www.pga.com/archive/pga-and-usga-step-new-sets-tees-in-nationwide-tee-it-forward-initiative.
8. Harriett Shephard, "Annabel Dimmock on Why Golfers Can Be Mean," *Women & Golf*, September 29, 2020, https://womenandgolf.com/news/women-and-golf-features/annabel-dimmock-on-why-golfers-can-be-mean.
9. Andrew McCarty, "Paige Spiranac Reveals What She Goes Through at Golf Courses," *The Spun by Sports Illustrated*, May 5, 2021, https://thespun.com/more/golf/paige-spiranac-reveals-what-she-goes-through-at-golf-courses.
10. Lex Pryor, "Golf's Historic Problems with Race Aren't Getting Better," *The Ringer*, April 7, 2021, https://www.theringer.com/2021/4/7/22370057/golf-diversity-issues-history-pga-lpga-the-masters.
11. Sarah J. Gervais, Theresa K. Vescio, and Jill Allen, "When What You See Is What You Get: The Consequences of the Objectifying Gaze for Women and Men," *Psychology of Women Quarterly* 35, no. 1 (March 2011): 5–17, https://doi.org/10.1177/0361684310386121.
12. Lara Winn and Randolph Cornelius, "Self-Objectification and Cognitive Performance: A Systematic Review of the Literature," *Frontiers in Psychology* 11, no. 13 (March 2020): 1–13, https://doi.org/10.3389/fpsyg.2020.00020.
13. Rachel M. Calogero and John T. Jost, "Self-Subjugation among Women: Exposure to Sexist Ideology, Self-Objectification, and the Protective Function of the Need to Avoid Closure," *Journal of Personality and Social Psychology* 100, no. 2 (February 2011): 211–28, https://doi.org/10.1037/a0021864.
14. Filip Raes and J. Mark G. Williams, "The Relationship between Mindfulness and Uncontrollability of Ruminative Thinking," *Mindfulness* 1, no. 4 (December 2010): 199–203, https://doi.org/10.1007/s12671-010-0021-6.
15. "Appendix F: Establishing Par," United States Golf Association, accessed June 11, 2021, https://www.usga.org/content/usga/home-page/handicapping/roh/Content/rules/Appendix%20F%20Establishing%20Par.htm.
16. Keith Cullen, *The Evolution of Golf Course Design* (Melbourne: Full Swing Golf Publishing, 2018).
17. Debert Cook, "Joseph M. Bartholomew—First African American Golf Course Architect and Designer," *African American Golfer's Digest*, June 30, 2017, https://africanamericangolfersdigest.com/joe-bartholomew-a-black-golf-course-architect-designer-in-history/.
18. Patricia M. Doney and Joseph P. Cannon, "An Examination of the Nature of Trust in Buyer-Seller Relationships," *Journal of Marketing* 61, no. 2 (April 1997): 35–51.

19. Nick Lebredo, "A Leadership Growth Journey," *Strategic Finance*, May 1, 2018, https://sfmagazine.com/articles/2018/may/a-leadership-growth-journey/.

20. Damon Hack, "Decades after Casper's Victory, a Winning Strategy Endures," *The New York Times*, June 12, 2006, https://www.nytimes.com/2006/06/12/sports/golf/12casper.html accessed 6/13/2021.

5. Leadership in the Fairway

1. Timo Kaski, Jarkko Niemi, and Ellen Pullins, "Rapport Building in Authentic B2B Sales Interaction," *Industrial Marketing Management* 69, no. 2 (February 2018): 235–52, https://doi.org/10.1016/j.indmarman.2017.08.019.

2. Edward L. Glaeser et al., "Measuring Trust," *Quarterly Journal of Economics* 115, no. 3 (August 2000): 811–46, https://doi.org/10.1162/003355300554926.

3. David Marmaros and Bruce Sacerdote, "How Do Friendships Form?" *Quarterly Journal of Economics* 121, no. 1 (February 2006): 79–119, https://doi.org/10.1093/qje/121.1.79.

4. Katherine W. Phillips, Nancy P. Rothband, and Tracy L. Dumas, "To Disclose or Not to Disclose? Status Distance and Self-Disclosure in Diverse Environments," *Academy of Management Review* 34, no. 4 (October 2009): 710–32, https://doi.org/10.5465/amr.34.4.zok710.

5. Sarah Woods et al., "'I'm So Excited for You!' How an Enthusiastic Responding Intervention Enhances Close Relationships," *Journal of Social & Personal Relationships* 32, no. 1 (February 2015): 24–40, https://doi.org/10.1177/0265407514523545.

6. Patricia M. Doney and Joseph P. Cannon, "An Examination of the Nature of Trust in Buyer-Seller Relationships," *Journal of Marketing* 61, no. 2 (April 1997): 35–51, https://doi.org/10.1177/002224299706100203.

7. Kelley J. Main, Darren W. Dahl, and Peter R. Darke, "Deliberative and Automatic Bases of Suspicion: Empirical Evidence of the Sinister Attribution Error," *Journal of Consumer Psychology* 17, no. 1 (January 2007): 59–69, https://doi.org/10.1207/s15327663jcp1701_9.

8. Susan Sprecher, "Closeness and Other Affiliative Outcomes Generated from the Fast Friends Procedure: A Comparison with a Small-Talk Task and Unstructured Self-Disclosure and the Moderating Role of Mode of Communication," *Journal of Social & Personal Relationships* 38, no. 5 (May 2021): 1452–71, https://doi.org/10.1177/0265407521996055.

9. Megan H. McCarthy, Joanne V. Wood, and John G. Holmes, "Dispositional Pathways to Trust: Self-Esteem and Agreeableness Interact to Predict Trust and Negative Emotional Disclosure," *Journal of Personality & Social Psychology* 113, no. 1 (July 2017): 95–116, https://doi.org/10.1037/pspi0000093.

10. Andrew Wright, "How to Calculate Distance in the Wind," *Golf Monthly*, March 5, 2021, https://www.golfmonthly.com/tips/golf-swing/how-to-calculate-distance-in-the-wind-108215.

11. Butch Harmon, "Four Shots for Beating the Slope," *Golf Digest*, February 27, 2011, https://www.golfdigest.com/story/butch-harmon-uneven-lies.

12. "Driving Distance vs. Fairways Hit," Imgur, August 20, 2017, https://imgur.com/BCGFJzy.

13. Luke Kerr-Dineen, "What Is a 'Flier'? How to Spot (and Master) One of the Trickiest Shots in Golf," *Golf*, July 11, 2020, https://golf.com/instruction/what-is-flier-lie-golf/.

14. Keely Levins, "These Two Mistakes Are Preventing You from Getting Out of Thick Rough," *Golf Digest*, June 16, 2017, https://www.golfdigest.com/story/these-two-mistakes-are-preventing-you-from-getting-out-of-thick-rough.

15. Jack Nicklaus, "Recovery Shots: Know When to Take the Risk," *Golf Digest*, December 10, 2015, https://www.golfdigest.com/story/jack-nicklaus-on-recovery-shots-know-when-to-take-the-risk.

16. Alexander Green, Nick Draper, and William Helton, "The Impact of Fear Words in a Secondary Task on Complex Motor Performance: A Dual-Task Climbing Study," *Psychological Research* 78, no. 4 (July 2014): 557–65, https://doi.org/10.1007/s00426-013-0506-8.

17. David Herrero-Fernández, "Psychophysiological, Subjective and Behavioral Differences Between High and Low Anger Drivers in a Simulation Task," *Transportation Research* 42, no. 2 (July 2016): 365–75, https://doi.org/10.1016/j.trf.2015.12.015; Oriana R. Aragón and John A. Bargh, "'So Happy I Could Shout!' and 'So Happy I Could Cry!' Dimorphous Expressions Represent and Communicate Motivational Aspects of Positive Emotions," *Cognition & Emotion* 32, no. 2 (March 2018): 286–302, https://doi.org/10.1080/02699931.2017.1301388.

18. Dwayne D. Gremler and Kevin P. Gwinner, "Customer-Employee Rapport in Service Relationships," *Journal of Service Research* 3, no. 1 (August 2000): 82–104, https://doi.org/10.1177/109467050031006.

19. Thomas Kilian, Sascha Steinmann, and Eva Hammes, "Oh My Gosh, I Got to Get Out of This Place! A Qualitative Study of Vicarious Embarrassment in Service Encounters," *Psychology & Marketing* 35, no. 1 (January 2018): 79-95, https://doi.org/10.1002/mar.21072.

20. Matthew Rudy, "Golf's Slow-Play Problem Explained: Top Instructors on the Root of the Problem and How to Fix It," *Golf Digest*, August 15, 2019, https://www.golfdigest.com/story/golfs-slow-play-problem-explained-top-instructors-on-the-root-of-the-problem-and-how-to-fix-it.

21. Max Adler, "The Real Cause of Slow Play Isn't What You Think," *Golf Digest*, November 17, 2014, https://www.golfdigest.com/story/the-real-cause-of-slow-play-is.

22. Adler.

23. "Breaking Down Barriers to Golf Participation," National Golf Foundation, October 15, 2019, https://www.ngf.org/breaking-down-barriers-to-golf-participation/.

24. Brian W. Swider, Murray R. Barrick, and Brad T. Harris, "Initial Impressions: What They Are, What They Are Not, and How They Influence Structured Interview Outcomes," *Journal of Applied Psychology* 101, no. 5 (May 2016): 625–38, https://doi.org/10.1037/apl0000077.

25. "Major Change: Encouraging Prompt Pace of Play," United States Golf Association, accessed June 17, 2021, https://www.usga.org/content/usga/home-page/rules-hub/rules-modernization/major-changes/encouraging-prompt-pace-of-play.html.

26. "Major Change: 'Maximum Score' Form of Stroke Play," United States Golf Association, accessed June 17, 2021, https://www.usga.org/content/usga/home-page/rules-hub/rules-modernization/major-changes/maximum-score--form-of-stroke-play.html.

27. "Double-Par Pickup Rule," StatMasters, accessed June 17, 2021, http://www.leaderboard.com/glossary_doubleparpickup.

28. Randy Chang, "How to Hit the Water Blast," *GolfTips*, May 25, 2017, https://www.golftipsmag.com/instruction/strategy-troubleshooting/hit-water-blast/.

6. Leadership at the Green

1. Brent Kelley, "Why Is the Golf Hole Size 4.25 Inches in Diameter?" SaddleBrooke Women's Golf Association, last modified March 9, 2017, https://www.sbwga.com/uploads/1/2/0/6/12060871/why_is_the_golf_hole_size_4.pdf.

2. Amy Mills, "LPGA70 Holes-In-One," Ladies Professional Golfers Association, April 20, 2020, https://www.lpga.com/news/2020/lpga70-holes-in-one.

3. "Charlie Sifford: A Hard Road to Golf Glory," United States Golf Association, February 3, 2019, https://www.usga.org/articles/2012/02/a-hard-road-to-golf-glory-21474845949.html.

4. Charlie Sifford, *Just Let Me Play: The Story of Charlie Sifford, the First Black PGA Golfer* (New York: British American Publishing, 1992).

5. Tiger Woods and Lorne Rubenstein, *The 1997 Masters: My Story* (New York: Grand Central Publishing, 2017).

6. Thomas Petersson, "What Is a Good Putting Average?" Anova Golf, January 21, 2020, https://anova.golf/what-is-a-good-putting-average/.

7. Petersson.

8. Zephyr Melton, "This Fascinating Chart Shows How Likely You Are to 3-Putt," *Golf*, May 4, 2020, https://golf.com/instruction/putting/fascinating-chart-shows-how-likely-three-putt/.

9. Erik J. Barzeski, "PGA Tour Putts Gained/Make Percentage Stats," *The Sand Trap*, July 24, 2011, https://thesandtrap.com/forums/topic/51757-pga-tour-putts-gainedmake-percentage-stats/.

10. Lawrence Smelser, "Average Golf Score," *Golfible*, last updated May 10, 2021, https://golfible.com/average-golf-score/.

11. Naomi K. Grant, Leandre R. Fabrigar, and Heidi Lim, "Exploring the Efficacy of Compliments as a Tactic for Securing Compliance," *Basic & Applied Social Psychology* 32, no. 3 (August 2010): 226–33, https://doi.org/10.1080/01973533.2010.497456.

12. David Drachman, Andre deCarufel, and Chester A. Insko, "The Extra Credit Effect in Interpersonal Attraction," *Journal of Experimental Social Psychology* 14, no. 5 (September 1978): 458–65, https://doi.org/10.1016/0022-1031(78)90042-2.

13. Thomas A. Nikolai, "Up to Speed: A Brief History of Green Speed," GCM, accessed June 22, 2021, https://www.gcmonline.com/course/environment/news/green-speed-history.

14. Matt Chivers, "Green Speeds: What's the Quickest Green You Have Ever Putted On?" *Golf Magic*, April 25, 2021, https://www.golfmagic.com/course-news/green-speeds-whats-quickest-green-you-have-ever-putted.

15. Kellie Stenzel, "6 Keys to Putting Ultra-Fast Greens, According to a Top 100 Teacher," *Golf*, April 11, 2021, https://golf.com/instruction/putting/6-keys-to-putting-ultra-fast-greens/.

16. Alison Wood Brooks, Francesca Gino, and Maurice E. Schweitzer, "Smart People Ask for (My) Advice: Seeking Advice Boosts Perceptions of Competence," *Management Science* 61, no. 6 (June 2015): 1421–35, https://doi.org/10.1287/mnsc.2014.2054.

17. Emma Levine and David Munguia Gomez, " 'I'm Just Being Honest.' When and Why Honesty Enables Help Versus Harm," *Journal of Personality and Social Psychology* 120, no. 1 (January 2021): 33–56, https://doi.org/10.1037/pspi0000242.

18. Brooks, Gino, and Schweitzer.

19. "Greens in Regulation Percentage," PGA Tour, accessed June 20, 221, https://www.pgatour.com/korn-ferry-tour/stats/stat.103.html.

20. "Golf Tips: Are You Hitting Enough Greens in Regulation? Improve Your Golf Handicap," *The Range*, March 19, 2013, https://www.thegrint.com/range/2013/03/golf-tips-gir/.

21. Ronald E. Smith et al., "Humor, Anxiety, and Task Performance," *Journal of Personality and Social Psychology* 19, no. 2 (August 1971): 243–46, https://doi.org/10.1037/h0031305.

22. Andrea B. Horn et al., "Positive Humor in Couples as Interpersonal Emotion Regulation: A Dyadic Study in Everyday Life on the Mediating Role of Psychological Intimacy," *Journal of Social and Personal Relationships* 36, no. 8 (July 2019): 2376–96, https://doi.org/10.1177/0265407518788197.

23. Horn et al.

24. Eric J. Romero and Kevin W. Cruthirds, "The Use of Humor in the Workplace," The *Academy of Management Perspectives* 20, no. 2 (May 2006): 58–69, https://doi.org/10.5465/amp.2006.20591005.

25. Bruce J. Avolio, Jane M. Howell, and John J. Sosik, "A Funny Thing Happened on the Way to the Bottom Line: Humor as a Moderator of Leadership Style Effects," *Academy of Management Journal* 42, no. 2 (November 1999): 219–27, https://doi.org/10.5465/257094.

26. "Rules Corner: What Are Some of the New Rules on the Putting Green?" *Golf*, April 11, 2020, https://golf.com/instruction/rules/what-are-some-new-rules-on-putting-green/.

27. Robert Lee, "If You Are off the Green but Closer to the Hole, Do You Putt First?" *SportsRec*, March 17, 2016, https://www.sportsrec.com/13733108/off-green-but-closer-hole-putt-first-20636html.

28. Mike Stachura, "The Science behind Why the Flagstick Should Be Pulled 99.9 Percent of the Time," *Golf Digest*, April 16, 2019, https://www.golfdigest.com/story/the-science-behind-why-the-flagstick-should-be-pulled-999-percent-of-the-time.

29. "Rules Corner: What Are Some of the New Rules on the Putting Green?" *Golf*, April 11, 2020, https://golf.com/instruction/rules/what-are-some-new-rules-on-putting-green/.

7. Leadership at the Nineteenth Hole

1. Pascal Tréguer, "'The Nineteenth Hole': Meaning and Early Occurrences," *word histories*, accessed June 26, 2021, https://wordhistories.net/2021/02/09/nineteenth-hole/.

2. Gavin Newsham, "Inside the Secretive World of America's Men-Only Golf Clubs," *New York Post*, May 22, 2021, https://nypost.com/article/inside-americas-men-only-golf-clubs/.

3. Michael McCann, "Why Private Golf Clubs Are Legally Still Able to Discriminate against Women," *Sports Illustrated*, July 1, 2019, https://www.si.com/golf-archives/2019/07/01/private-golf-clubs-muirfield-augusta-women-discrimination.

4. Timo Kaski, Jarkko Niemi, and Ellen Pullins, "Rapport Building in Authentic B2B Sales Interaction," *Industrial Marketing Management* 69, no. 2 (February 2018): 235–52, https://doi.org/10.1016/j.indmarman.2017.08.019.

5. Penelope Lockwood, Chritsian H. Jordan, and Ziva Kunda, "Motivation by Positive or Negative Role Models: Regulatory Focus Determines Who Will Best Inspire Us," *Journal of Personality and Social Psychology* 83, no. 4 (October 2002): 854–64, https://doi.org/10.1037/0022-3514.83.4.854.

6. Harry T. Reis and Philip Shaver, "Intimacy as an Interpersonal Process," in *Handbook of Personal Relationships: Theory, Research and Interventions*, ed. Steve Duck et al. (New York: John Wiley & Sons, 1988), 367–89.

7. Sharon K. Parker and Carolyn M. Axtell, "Seeing Another Viewpoint: Antecedents and Outcomes of Employee Perspective Taking," *Academy of Management Journal* 44, no. 6 (December 2001): 1085–100, https://doi.org/10.5465/3069390.

8. Sara B. Algoe, "Find, Remind, and Bind: The Functions of Gratitude in Everyday Relationships," *Social and Personality Psychology Compass* 6, no. 6 (June 2012): 455–69, https://doi.org/10.1111/j.1751-9004.2012.00439.x.

9. Robert B. Cialdini and Brad Sagarin, "Principles of Interpersonal Influence," in *Persuasion: Psychological Insights and Perspectives*, ed. Timothy C. Brock and Melanie C. Green (New York: Sage Publications, 2005), 143–69.

10. Albert Mehrabian and Shirley G. Diamond, "Seating Arrangement and Conversation," *Sociometry* 34, no. 2 (June 1971): 281–89, https://doi.org/10.2307/2786417.

11. Antonia Abbey, "Alcohol-Related Sexual Assault: A Common Problem among College Students," *Journal of Studies on Alcohol and Drugs* 14, no. 1 (March 2002): 118–28, https://doi.org/10.15288/jsas.2002.s14.118.

12. Natalie Lundsteen, "When Your Career Path Intersects with Alcohol," *Inside Higher Ed*, February 25, 2019, https://www.insidehighered.com/advice/2019/02/25/knowing-when-drink-alcohol-and-how-much-professional-events-opinion.

13. Charles Spence and Xiaoang Wan, "Beverage Perception and Consumption: The Influence of the Container on the Perception of the Contents," *Food Quality and Preference* 39, no. 1 (January 2015): 131–40, https://doi.org/10.1016/j.foodqual.2014.07.007.

14. Stephanie L. Brown, Terrilee Asher, and Robert B. Cialdini, "Evidence of a Positive Relationship between Age and Preference for Consistency," *Journal of Research in Personality* 39, no. 5 (October 2005): 517–33, https://doi.org/10.1016/j.jrp.2020.104014.

15. Richard F. Beltramini, "Exploring the Effectiveness of Business Gifts: A Controlled Field Experiment," *Journal of the Academy of Marketing Science* 20, no. 1 (December 1992): 87–91, https://doi.org/10.1007/BF02723479.

8. Heading Back to the Office

1. Dawnet Beverley, "Golf as a Tool for Executive Leadership Development" (MA diss., Graziadio Business School, 2014), 449.

2. Paul L. Nesbit, "The Role of Self-Reflection, Emotional Management of Feedback, and Self-Regulation Processes in Self-Directed Leadership Development," *Human Resource Development Review* 11, no. 2 (April 2012): 203–26, https://doi.org/10.1177/1534484312439196.

3. Marilyn W. Daudelin, "Learning from Experience through Reflection," *Organizational Dynamics* 24, no. 3 (December 1996): 36–48, https://doi.org/10.1016/S0090-2616(96)90004-2.

4. Giada Di Stefano et al., "Making Experience Count: The Role of Reflection in Individual Learning," *Harvard Business School Working Paper* 14, no. 93 (March 2014): 39, https://doi.org/10.2139/ssrn.2414478.

5. Sonja Lyubomirsky, Lorie Sousa, and Rene Dickerhoof, "The Costs and Benefits of Writing, Talking and Thinking about Life's Triumphs and Defeats," *Journal of Personality and Social Psychology* 90, no. 4 (April 2006): 692–708, https://doi.org/10.1037/0022-3514.90.4.692.

6. J. Gregory Hixon and William B. Swann Jr., "When Does Introspection Bear Fruit? Self-Reflection, Self-Insight, and Interpersonal Choices," *Journal of Personality and Social Psychology* 64, no. 1 (February 1993): 34–43, https://doi.org/10.1037/0022-3514.64.1.35.

7. Jefferson A. Singer, "Narrative Identity and Meaning Making across the Adult Lifespan: An Introduction," *Journal of Personality* 72, no. 3 (April 2004): 437–59, https://doi.org/10.1111/j.0022-3506.2004.00268.x.

8. "NGF Golf Instruction Report Overview," National Golf Foundation, accessed July 18, 2021, https://www.ngf.org/ngf-releases-golf-instruction-report/.

9. "Become an LPGA Certified Teacher," LPGA, accessed July 5, 2021, https://www.lpga.com/lpga-professionals/home-become-a-member; "How to Become a PGA Member," PGA, accessed July 5, 2021, https://www.pga.org/membership/.

10. "How Much Do Golf Lessons Cost?" *Back 2 Basics Golf*, October 13, 2020, https://back2basics.golf/blogs/news/how-much-do-golf-lessons-cost.

11. Altaf Merchant, John B. Ford, and Adrian Sargeant, "'Don't Forget to Say Thank You': The Effect of an Acknowledgement on Donor Relationships," *Journal of Marketing Management* 26, nos. 7–8 (July 2010): 593–611, https://doi.org/10.1080/02672571003780064.

12. Merchant, Ford, and Sargeant.

13. Barbara Stiglbauer and Silvana Weber, "A Picture Paints a Thousand Words: The Influence of Taking Selfies on Place Identification," *Journal of Environmental Psychology* 58 (August 2018): 18–26, https://doi.org/10.1016/j.jenvp.2018.07.007.

14. Duane M. Nagel et al., "Purchaser Perceptions of Early Phase Supplier Relationships: The Role of Similarity and Likeability," *Journal of Business Research* 128, no. 5 (May 2021): 174–86, https://doi.org/10.1016/j.jbusres.2021.01.026.

15. Ruoxu Wang, Fan Yang, and Michel M. Haigh, "Let Me Take a Selfie: Exploring the Psychological Effects of Posting and Viewing Selfies and Groupies on Social Media," *Telematics and Informatics* 34, no. 4 (July 2017): 274–83, https://doi.org/10.1016/j.tele.2016.07.004.

16. Kirsten Martin, "The Penalty for Privacy Violations: How Privacy Violations Impact Trust Online," *Journal of Business Research* 82, no. 1 (January 2018): 103–16, https://doi.org/10.1016/j.jbusres.2017.08.034.

17. Gunter Bahr and Till Requate, "Reciprocity and Giving in a Consecutive Three-Person Dictator Game with Social Interaction," *German Economic Review* 15, no. 3 (August 2014): 374–92, https://doi.org/10.1111/geer.12013.

18. "How Much Does Leadership Training Cost?" *Rapport*, September 16, 2019, https://blog.rapportleadership.com/how-much-does-leadership-training-cost.

19. Sherwin Rosen, "Human Capital," in *Social Economics*, ed. John Eatwell, Murray Milgate, and Peter Newman (London: Palgrave Macmillan, 1989), 136–55.

20. Charles H. Schwepker Jr. and Roberta J. Schultz, "Influence of the Ethical Servant Leader and Ethical Climate on Customer Value Enhancing Sales Performance," *Journal of Personal Selling and Sales Management* 35, no. 2 (February 2015): 93–107, https://doi.org/10.1080/08853134.2015.1010537; Friederike Gerlach, Maike Hundeling, and Kathrin Rosing, "Ambidextrous Leadership and Innovation Performance: A Longitudinal Study," *Leadership & Organization Development Journal* 41, no. 3 (May 2020): 383–98, https://doi.org/10.1108/LODJ-07-2019-0321.

21. Mike Prokopeak, "Follow the Leader(ship) Spending," *Chief Learning Officer*, March 21, 2018, https://www.chieflearningofficer.com/2018/03/21/follow-the-leadership-spending/.

22. James S. Coleman, "Social Capital in the Creation of Human Capital," *American Journal of Sociology* 94 (1988): 95–120, https://doi.org/10.1086/228943.

23. Kristi Dosh, "Golfers Make Better Business Executives," *Forbes*, May 16, 2016, https://www.forbes.com/sites/kristidosh/2016/05/16/golfers-make-better-business-executives/?sh=694b8fc0b4a5.

24. Sumit Agarwal et al., "Playing the Boys Game: Golf Buddies and Board Diversity," *American Economic Review* 106, no. 5 (May 2016): 272–76, https://doi.org/10.1257/aer.p20161033.

25. Jody Agius Vallejo, "Socially Mobile Mexican Americans and the Minority Culture of Mobility," *American Behavioral Scientist* 56, no. 5 (2012): 666–81, https://doi.org/10.1177/0002764211433807.

26. Steve Milano, "The Advantages of Sitting on a Board of Directors," *Career Trend*, last modified July 5, 2017, https://careertrend.com/13360019/the-advantages-of-sitting-on-a-board-of-directors.

27. Steven Boivie et al., "Serving on Boards Helps Executives Get Promoted," *Harvard Business Review*, May 20, 2016, https://hbr.org/2016/05/serving-on-boards-helps-executives-get-promoted.

28. O. C. Ferrell et al., "Business Ethics, Corporate Social Responsibility, and Brand Attitudes: An Exploratory Study," *Journal of Business Research* 95, no. 1 (February 2018): 491–501, https://doi.org/10.1016/j.jbusres.2018.07.039.

29. Christopher J. Waples and Benjamin J. Brachle, "Recruiting Millennials: Exploring the Impact of CSR Involvement and Pay Signaling on Organizational Attractiveness," *Corporate Social Responsibility and Environmental Management* 27, no. 2 (March/April 2019): 870–80, https://doi.org/10.1002/csr.1851.

30. Joe Beditz, "Women in Golf: Progress and Opportunity," *National Golf Foundation*, June 3, 2021, https://www.ngf.org/women-in-golf-progress-and-opportunity/.

31. Steve Keating, "Diversity Remains Golf's Biggest Challenge, Says PGA of America CEO," *Reuters*, August 9, 2018, https://www.reuters.com/article/us-golf-pgachamp-diversity/diversity-remains-golfs-biggest-challenge-says-pga-of-america-ceo-idUSKBN1KT2OE.

32. Carolyn Y. Nicholson, Larry D. Compeau, and Rajesh Sethi, "The Role of Interpersonal Liking in Building Trust in Long-Term Channel Relationships," *Journal of the Academy of Marketing Science* 29, no. 1 (December 2001): 3–15, https://doi.org/10.1177/0092070301291001.

33. Robert M. Morgan and Shelby D. Hunt, "The Commitment-Trust Theory of Relationship Marketing," *Journal of Marketing* 58, no. 3 (July 1994): 20–38, https://doi.org/10.2307/1252308.

34. Ronald S. Burt, Martin Kilduff, and Stefano Tasselli, "Social Network Analysis: Foundations and Frontiers on Advantage," *Annual Review of Psychology* 64, no. 1 (January 2013): 527–47, https://doi.org/10.1146/annurev-psych-113011-143828.

35. Oberiri Destiny Apuke and Bahiyah Omar, "What Drives News Sharing Behaviour Among Social Media Users? A Relational Communication Model from the Social Capital Perspective," *International Sociology* 36, no. 3 (May 2021): 339–61, https://doi.org/10.1177/0268580920961323.

9. Leadership and Golf for Life

1. Will Gray, "Report: 'Off-Course' Participation Fuels Golf Growth," *Golf Channel*, April 25, 2017, https://www.golfchannel.com/article/golf-central-blog/report-course-participation-fuels-golf-growth.
2. Adam Stanley, "Off-Course Golf: How Big Can It Get?" National Golf Foundation, May 9, 2021, https://www.ngf.org/off-course-golf-how-big-can-it-get/.
3. Wayne E. Baker and Nathaniel Bulkley, "Paying it Forward vs. Rewarding Reputation: Mechanisms of Generalized Reciprocity," *Organizational Science* 25, no. 5 (June 2014): 1493–510, https://doi.org/10.1287/orsc.2014.0920.
4. Brent Simpson et al., "The Roots of Reciprocity: Gratitude and Reputation in Generalized Exchange Systems," *American Sociological Review* 83, no. 1 (December 2018): 88–110, https://doi.org/10.1177/0003122417747290.

Index

About the Authors

Dr. Eric Boyd is the cofounder of FairWays to Leadership. He is an associate professor of marketing at the University of Central Florida where he teaches marketing and sales in the DeVos Sport Business Management program. Eric is also emeritus professor of marketing at James Madison University and serves as honorary visiting professor at the University of Edinburgh in Scotland. He is an award-winning teacher and researcher whose research has appeared in leading business publications, including *Harvard Business Review* and *Advertising Age*. Eric received his PhD from the University of Virginia.

Anna Alvarez Boyd is the cofounder of FairWays to Leadership. She brings over twenty-five years of diverse experience as a senior leader in government, corporate, and nonprofit sectors, where she led housing, mortgage finance, and community development policy at a national level. Anna is also founder of Executive Horizons LLC, a consulting and leadership coaching business. She is an Associate Certified Coach (ACC) and graduate of Georgetown University's Transformational Leadership Coaching program. She is an International Coaching Federation member.